I AM

COME AND KNOW JESUS BETTER

DAVID MALANDER

ARPress
ILLUMINATING IDEAS
EMPOWERING VOICES

ARPress
45 Dan Road Suite 36
Canton MA 02021

Hotline: 1(800) 220-7660
Fax: 1(855) 752-6001

Ordering Information:
Quantity Sales. Special discounts are available on quantity purchases by corporations, associations, and others. For details, contact the publisher at the address above.

Printed in the United States of America.

ISBN-13	Softcover	979-8-89676-504-2
	eBook	979-8-89676-505-9
	Hardback	979-8-89676-506-6

Library of Congress Control Number: 2019918641

Biographies

I being a Born again follower of Jesus Christ I was born in 1958 raised in a Christian family. Which helped me on the way to knowing the Lord. I gave my life to him when I was eight teen. With trials and hardships along the way, He saw me through. For he gave me a Love for his word and a desire to share it with whosoever would listen.

I married a wonderful Christian help mate in ninety four who has helped me complete this manuscript of Jesus life. Combining the four Gospels into a complete story of the Birth life, ministry trial crucifixion death and reassertion Of Jesus Our Saver.

My hope is that as many who would read this will know what a mighty work God has done for us by sending his only Son and by giving up his life on the cross for our sins. He made a pathway to Heaven for us. That we may be saved from the condemnation and Hell our sinful nature deserves. For we have all sinned and fell sort of the commandments of God. For as the Holy word says we are all eternal beings and where we chose to spend it after we die is our chose. For Jesus said I am the way the truth and the life, who should ever believe in me will have eternal life.

If the Lord has touched your heart after reading this his word. And you seek to known him better; Ask him to forgive your sins and to send His Holy Spirit into your Heart. And He who is faithful and true will hear your prayer. Then just open the bible in prayer and see for yourself our past, present, and future.

Sincerely servant of the King
David Malander

I "AM"

According to Matthew, Mark, Luke, and John

*F*orasmuch as many have taken in hand to set forth in order a declaration of those things which are most surely true, even as they were delivered unto us, by the apostles, which from the beginning were eyewitnesses, and ministers of the word and inspired by the ***Holy Spirit***.

In the Beginning Was the Word

And the Word was with God, and the Word was God. The same was in the beginning with God. All things were made by him; and without him was not anything made that was made. In him was life; and the life was the light of men. And the light shineth in darkness; and the darkness comprehended it not.

There was a man sent from God, whose name was John. The same came for a witness, to bear witness of the light, that Jesus was the true light, which lighteth every man that cometh into the world, that all men through him might believe. He was not that light, but was sent to bear witness of that light. He was in the world, and the world was made by him, and the world knew him not. He came unto his own, and his own received him not. But as many as received him, to them gave he power to become the sons of God, even to them that believe on his name. Which were born, not of blood, nor of the will of the flesh, nor of the will of man, but of God. And the Word was made flesh, and dwelt among us, and we beheld his glory, the glory as of the only begotten of the Father (full of grace and truth).

Ancestors of Jesus

The book of the genealogies of Jesus Christ, the son of David, the son of Abraham. Abraham begat Isaac; and Isaac begat Jacob; and Jacob begat Judah and his brethren; And Judah begat Phares and Zara of Thamar; and Phares begat Esrom; and Esrom begat Aram; And Aram begat Aminadab; and Aminadab begat Naasson; and Naasson begat Salmon;

And Salmon begat Boaz of Rachab; and Boaz begat Obed of Ruth; and Obed begat Jesse; And Jesse begat David the king; and David the king begat Solomon of her that had been the wife of Urias; And Solomon begat Roboam; and Roboam begat Abia; and Abia begat Asa; And Asa begat Josaphat; and Josaphat begat Joram; and Joram begat Ozias; And Ozias begat Joatham; and Joatham begat Achaz; and Achaz begat Ezekias; And Ezekias begat Manasses; and Manasses begat Amon; and Amon begat Josias; And Josias begat Jechonias and his brethren, about the time they were carried away to Babylon:

And after they were brought to Babylon, Jechonias begat Salathiel; and Salathiel begat Zorobabel; And Zorobabel begat Abiud; and Abiud begat Eliakim; and Eliakim begat Azor; And Azor begat Sadoc; and Sadoc begat Achim; and Achim begat Eliud; And Eliud begat Eleazar; and Eleazar begat Matthan; and Matthan begat Jacob;

And Jacob begat Joseph the husband of Mary, of whom was born Jesus, who is called Christ. So all the generations from Abraham to David are fourteen generations; and from David until the carrying away into Babylon are fourteen generations; and from the carrying away into Babylon unto Christ *are* fourteen generations.

Angel Promises the Birth of John to Zacharias

There was in the days of Herod, the king of Judaea, a certain priest named Zacharias, of the course of Abia: and his wife was of the daughters of Aaron, and her name was Elisabeth. And they were both righteous before God, walking in all the commandments and ordinances of the Lord blameless. And they had no child, because that Elisabeth was barren, and they both were now well stricken in years.

And it came to pass, that while he executed the priest's office before God in the order of his course, according to the custom of the priest's office, his lot was to burn incense when he went into the temple of the Lord. And the whole multitude of the people were praying without at the time of incense. And there appeared unto him an angel of the Lord standing on the right side of the altar of incense. And when Zacharias saw him, he was troubled, and fear fell upon him. But the angel said unto him, *Fear not, Zacharias: for thy prayer is heard; and thy wife Elisabeth shall bear thee a son, and thou shalt call his name John. And thou shalt have joy and gladness; and many shall rejoice at his birth. For he shall be great in the sight of the Lord, and shall drink neither wine nor strong drink; and he shall be filled with the Holy Ghost, even from his mother's womb.*

And many of the children of Israel shall he turn unto to the Lord their God.

And he shall go before him in the spirit and power of Elias and turn the hearts of fathers to their children, and the disobedient to the wisdom of the just; to make ready a people prepared for the Lord.

And Zacharias said unto the angel, Whereby shall I know this? for I am an old man, and my wife well stricken in years. And the angel answering said unto him, *I am Gabriel, that stand in the presence of God; and am sent to speak unto thee, and to show thee these glad tidings. And, behold, thou shalt be dumb, and not able to speak, until the day that these things shall be performed, because thou believest not my words, which shall be fulfilled in their season.*

And the people waited for Zacharias, and marveled that he tarried so long in the temple. And when he came out, he could not speak unto them: and they perceived that he had seen a vision in the temple: then he beckoned unto them, and remained speechless. And it came to pass, that, as soon as the days of his ministration were accomplished, he departed to his own house. And after those days his wife Elisabeth conceived, and hid herself five months, saying, *Thus hath the Lord dealt with me in the days wherein he looked on me, to take away my reproach among men;*

THE SALUTATION OF MARY

And in the sixth month the angel Gabriel was sent from God unto a city of Galilee, named Nazareth, to a virgin espoused to a man whose name was Joseph, of the house of David; and the virgin's name was Mary. And the angel came unto her, and said, *Hail, thou that art highly favored, the Lord is with thee: blessed art thou among women.* And when she saw him, she was troubled at his saying, and cast in her mind what manner of salutation this should be. And the angel said unto her*, Fear not, Mary: for thou hast found favor with God. And, behold, thou shalt conceive within thy womb, and bring forth a son, and shalt call his name JESUS. He shall be great, and shall be called the Son of the Most Highest: and the Lord God shall give unto him the throne of his father David: And he shall reign over the house of Jacob forever; and of his kingdom there shall be no end.*

Then said Mary unto the angel, *how shall this be, seeing I know not a man?* And the angel answered and said unto her*, The Holy Ghost shall come upon thee, and the power of the Most High shall overshadow thee: therefore also that Holy child which shall be born of thee shall be called the Son of God. And, behold, thy cousin Elisabeth, who was called barren; she hath also conceived a son in her old age: and this is the sixth month with her. For with God nothing shall be impossible.* And Mary said, *Behold the handmaid of the Lord, be it unto me according to thy word.* And the angel departed from her.

Mary Visits Elisabeth

And Mary arose in those days, and went into the hill country with haste, into a city of Judea; and entered into the house of Zacharias, and saluted Elisabeth. And it came to pass, that, when Elisabeth heard the salutation of Mary, the babe leaped within her womb; and Elisabeth was filled with the **Holy Ghost:** And she spake out with a loud voice, and said, *Blessed art thou among women, and blessed is the fruit of thy womb. And whence is this to me, that the mother of my Lord should come to me? And blessed is she that believed: for there shall be a performance of those things which were told her from the Lord.*

*And **Mary** said, **My soul doth magnify the Lord, and my spirit hath rejoiced in God my Savior. For he hath regarded the low estate of his handmaiden: for, behold, from henceforth all generations shall call me blessed.***

For he that is mighty hath done to me great things; and holy is his name. And his mercy is on them that fear him from generation to generation. He hath showed strength with his arm; he hath scattered the proud in the imagination of their hearts. He hath put down the mighty from their seats, and exalted them of low degree. He hath filled the hungry with good things; and the rich he hath sent away empty. He hath helped his servant Israel, in remembrance of his mercy; as he spake to our fathers, to Abraham and to his seed forever. And Mary abode with her about three months, and returned to her own house.

The Birth of John the Baptist

Now Elisabeth's full time came that she should be delivered; and she brought forth a son. And her neighbors and her cousins heard how the Lord had showed great mercy upon her; and they rejoiced with her.

And it came to pass, that on the eighth day they came to circumcise the child; and they called him Zacharias, after the name of his father. And his mother answered and said, *Not so; he shall be called John.* And they said unto her, there is none of thy kindred that is called by this name. And they made signs to his father, how he would have him called. And he asked for a writing table, and wrote, saying, His name is *John.* And they marveled all. And his mouth was opened immediately, and his tongue loosed, and he spoke, and praised God. And fear came on all that dwelt round about them: and all these sayings were noised abroad throughout all the hill country of Judaea. And all they that heard them laid them up in their hearts, saying, What manner of child shall this be!

And the hand of the Lord was with him. And his father Zacharias was filled with the **Holy Ghost,** and prophesied, saying, *Blessed be the Lord of Israel: for he hath visited and redeemed his people, And hath raised up an horn of salvation for us in the house of his servant David; As he spake by the mouth of his holy prophets, which have been since the world began: That we should be saved from our enemies, and from the hand of all that hate us; To perform the mercy that was promised to our fathers, and to remember his holy covenant; The oath which he swore to our father Abraham, That he would grant unto us, that we being delivered out of the hand of our enemies might serve him without fear, In holiness* *and righteousness before him, all the days of our life. And thou, child, shalt be called the prophet of the Highest: for thou shalt go before the face of the Lord to prepare his ways; To give knowledge of salvation unto his people by remission of their sins, Through the tender mercy of our God; whereby the dayspring from on high hath visited us, To give light to them that sit in darkness and in the shadow of death, to guide our feet into the way of peace.* And the child grew, and waxed strong in spirit, and was in the deserts till the day of his showing unto Israel.

ANGEL APPEARS TO JOSEPH

Now the birth of Jesus Christ was on this wise: When as his mother Mary was espoused to Joseph, before they came together, she was found with child of the ***Holy Ghost.*** Then Joseph her husband, being a just man, and not willing to make her a public example, was minded to put her away privily. But while he thought on these things, behold, the angel of the Lord appeared unto him in a dream, saying, ***Joseph, thou son of David, fear not to take unto thee Mary thy wife: for that which is conceived in her is of the Holy Ghost. And she shall bring forth a son, and thou shalt call his name Jesus: for he shall save his people from their sins.*** Now all this was done, that it might be fulfilled which was spoken of the Lord by the prophet, saying, *Behold, a virgin shall be with child, and shall bring forth a son, and they shall call his name Emmanuel, which being interpreted is, God with us.* Then Joseph being raised from sleep did as the angel of the Lord had bidden him, and took unto him Mary as his wife: And knew her not till she had brought forth her firstborn son: and he called his name **Jesus.**

THE BIRTH OF JESUS

And it came to pass in those days, that there went out a decree from Caesar Augustus, that all the land should be taxed. (And this taxing was first made when Cyrenius was governor of Syria.) And all went to be taxed, every one into his own city. And Joseph also went up from Galilee, out of the city of Nazareth, into Judaea, unto the city of David, which is called Bethlehem; (because he was of the house and lineage of David:) To be taxed with Mary his espoused wife, being great with child. And so it was, that, while they were there, the days were accomplished that she should be delivered. And she brought forth her firstborn son, and wrapped him in swaddling clothes, and laid him in a manger; because there was no room for them in the inn.

Shepherds Visit Jesus

And there were in the same country shepherds abiding in the field, keeping watch over their flock by night. And, the angel of the Lord came upon them, and the glory of the Lord shone round about them: and they were sore afraid. And the angel said unto them, ***Fear not: for, behold, I bring you glad tidings of great joy, which shall be to all people. For unto you is born this day in the city of David a Savior, which is Christ the Lord. And this shall be a sign unto you; Ye shall find the babe wrapped in swaddling clothes, lying in a manger.*** *And suddenly there was with the angel a multitude of the heavenly host praising God, and saying,* ***Glory to God in the highest, and on earth peace, good will toward men.***

And it came to pass, as the angels were gone away from them into heaven, the shepherds said one to another, Let us now go even unto Bethlehem, and see this thing which is come to pass, which the Lord hath made known unto us. And they came with haste, and found Mary, and Joseph, and the babe lying in a manger. And when they had seen it, they made known abroad the saying which was told them concerning this child. And all they that heard it wondered at those things which were told them. by the shepherds. But Mary kept all these things, and pondered them in her heart. And the shepherds returned, glorifying and praising God for all the things that they had heard and seen, as it was told unto them.

Circumcision of Jesus

And when eight days were accomplished for the circumcising of the child, his name was called JESUS, which was so named of the angel before he was conceived in the womb. And when the days of her purification according to the Law of Moses were accomplished, they brought him to Jerusalem, to present him to the Lord; (As it is written in the law of the Lord, Every male that openeth the womb shall be called holy to the Lord;) And to offer a sacrifice according to that which is said in the law of the Lord, A pair of turtledoves, or two young pigeons.

And, behold, there was a man in Jerusalem, whose name was Simeon; and he was just and devout, waiting for the consolation of Israel: And the Holy Ghost was upon him. And it was revealed unto him by the Holy Ghost, that he should not see death, before he had seen the Lord's Christ. And he came by the Spirit into the temple: and when the parents brought in the child Jesus, to do for him after the custom of law.

Then took he him up in his arms, and blessed God, and said, *O Lord, now lettest thou thy servant depart in peace, according to thy word: For mine eyes have seen thy salvation, Which thou hast prepared before the face of all people; A light to lighten the Gentiles, and the glory of thy people Israel.* And Joseph and his mother marveled at those things which were spoken of him. And Simeon blessed them, and said unto Mary his mother, *Behold, this child is set for the fall and rising of many in Israel; and for a sign which shall be spoken against; (Yea, a sword shall pierce through thy own soul also,) that the thoughts of many hearts may be revealed.*

And there was one Anna, a prophetess, the daughter of Phanuel, of the tribe of Aser: she was of a great age, and had lived with her husband seven years from her virginity. And she was a widow of about fourscore and four years, which departed not from the temple, but served God with fasting and prayers night and day. And she coming in that instant gave thanks likewise unto the Lord, and spake of him to all them that looked for redemption in Jerusalem. And when they had performed all things according to the law of the Lord, they returned back to the Bethlehem there they were staying.

VISITORS FROM THE EAST

Now when Jesus was born in Bethlehem of Judaea in the days of Herod the king, behold, there came wise men from the east to Jerusalem, saying, Where is he that is born King of the Jews? For we have seen his star in the east, and are come to worship him. When Herod the king had heard these things, he was troubled, and all Jerusalem with him. And when he had gathered all the chief priests and scribes of the people together, he demanded of them where Christ should be born. And they said unto him, In Bethlehem of Judaea: for thus it is written by the prophet, *And thou Bethlehem, in the land of Juda, art not the least among the princes of Juda: for out of thee shall come a Governor, that shall rule my people Israel.*

Then Herod, when he had privily called the wise men, enquired of them diligently what time the star appeared. And he sent them to Bethlehem, and said, Go and search diligently for the young child; and when ye have found him, bring me word again, that I may come and worship him also. When they had heard the king, they departed; and, lo, the star, which they saw in the east, went before them, till it came and stood over where the young child was. When they saw the star, they rejoiced with exceeding great joy. And when they were come into the house, they saw the young child with Mary his mother, and fell down, and worshipped him: and when they had opened their treasures, they presented unto him gifts; gold, and frankincense, and myrrh. And being warned of God in a dream that they should not return to Herod, they departed into their own country another way.

Escape to Egypt
and Return to Nazareth

And when they were departed, behold, the angel of the Lord appeareth to Joseph in a dream, saying, *Arise, and take the young child and his mother, and flee into Egypt, and be thou there until I bring thee word: for Herod will seek the young child to destroy him.* When he arose, he took the young child and his mother by night, and departed into Egypt: And was there until the death of Herod: that it might be fulfilled which was spoken of the Lord by the prophet, saying, *Out of Egypt have I called my son.*

Then Herod, when he saw that he was mocked of the wise men, was exceeding wroth, and sent forth, and slew all the children that were in Bethlehem, and in all the coasts thereof, from two years old and under, according to the time which he had diligently inquired of the wise men. Then was fulfilled that which was spoken by Jeremiah the prophet, saying, *In Rama was there a voice heard, lamentation, and weeping, and great mourning, Rachel weeping for her children, and would not be comforted, because they are not.*

But when Herod was dead, behold, an angel of the Lord appeareth in a dream to Joseph in Egypt, saying, *Arise, and take the young child and his mother, and go into the land of Israel: for they are dead which sought the young child's life.* And he arose, and took the young child and his mother, and came into the land of Israel. But when he heard that Herod Archelaus did reign in Judaea in the room of his father Herod, he was afraid to go thither: notwithstanding, being warned of God in a dream, he turned aside into the parts of Galilee, to their own city Nazareth. And the child grew, and waxed strong in spirit, filled with wisdom: and the grace of God was upon him.

Jesus Speaks
with Religious Teachers

Now his parents went to Jerusalem every year at the feast of the Passover. And when he was twelve years old, they went up to Jerusalem after the custom of the feast. And when they had fulfilled the days, as they returned, the child Jesus tarried behind in Jerusalem; and Joseph and his mother knew not of *it*. But they, supposing him to have been in the company, went a day's journey; and they sought him among their kinsfolk and acquaintance. And when they found him not, they turned back again to Jerusalem, seeking him. And it came to pass, that after three days they found him in the temple, sitting in the midst of the doctors, both hearing them, and asking them questions. And all that heard him were astonished at his understanding and answers. And when they saw him, they were amazed: and his mother said unto him, Son, why hast thou thus dealt with us? Behold, thy father and I have sought thee sorrowing. And he said unto them, **How is it that ye sought me? Noest thou not that I must be about my Father's business?** And they understood not the saying which he spake unto them. And he went down with them, and came to Nazareth, and was subject unto them: but his mother kept all these sayings in her heart. And Jesus increased in wisdom and stature, and in favor with God and man.

John the Baptist Prepares the Way for Jesus

Now in the fifteenth year of the reign of Tiberius Caesar, Pontius Pilate being governor of Judaea, and Herod being tetrarch of Galilee, and his brother Philip tetrarch of Ituraea and of the region of Trachonitis, and Lysanias, the tetrarch of Abilene, Annas and Caiaphas being the high priests, the word of God came unto John the son of Zacharias in the wilderness.

And he came into all the country about the wilderness of Judaea, as it is written in the book of the words of Esaias the prophet, saying, *I send my Messenger, The voice of one crying in the wilderness, Prepare ye the way of the Lord, make his paths straight, Repent ye: for the kingdom of heaven is at hand. Every valley shall be filled, and every mountain and hill shall be brought low; and the crooked shall be made straight, and the rough ways shall be made smooth; And all flesh shall see the salvation of God.* For as John did baptize and preach the baptism of repentance for the remission of sins.

And there went out unto him in all the land, and they of Jerusalem, and were all baptized of him in the river of Jordan, confessing their sins. And John was clothed with camel's hair, and with a girdle of a skin about his loins; and he did eat locusts and wild honey; and preached, for the kingdom of heaven is at hand.

Then came onto him sent from the Jews, the priests and Levites from Jerusalem to ask him, Who art thou? Art thou Elias? And he saith, *I am not*, Art thou that prophet? And he answered, *No.* Then said they unto him, who art thou? that we may give an answer to them that sent us. What sayest thou of thyself?

And they which were sent were of the Pharisees. Asked again, and said unto him, Why baptizes thou then, if thou be not that Christ, nor Elias, neither that prophet? John answered them, saying, *I baptize with water: but there cometh one who already standeth among you, whom ye know not; He it is, who coming after me is preferred before me.*

Then said he to the multitude that came forth to be baptized of him,

O ye generation of vipers, who hath warned you to flee from the wrath to come? Bring forth therefore fruits worthy of repentance, and begin not to say within yourselves, We have Abraham as our Father: for I say unto you, That God is able of these stones to raise up children unto Abraham. And know whose fan is in his hand, and he will thoroughly purge his floor, and gather his wheat into the garner; also the ax is laid unto the root of the trees: every tree therefore which bringeth not forth good fruit is hewn down, and he will burn up the chaff with unquenchable fire. Then the people asked him, saying, what shall we do then? He answereth and saith unto them, *He that has two coats, impart to him that hath none; and he that hath meat, let him do likewise.*

Then came also publicans to be baptized, and said unto him, Master, what shall we do? And he said unto them, *Exact no more than that which is appointed to you.* And the soldiers likewise demanded of him, saying, And what shall we do? And he said unto them, *Do violence to no man, neither accuse any falsely; and be content with your wages.* And as the people were in expectation, and all men mused in their hearts of John, whether he were the Christ, or not; John answered, saying unto them all, *I am the voice of one crying in the wildness: But one mightier than I cometh, the latches of whose shoes I am not worthy to unloose: He shall baptize you with the* **Holy Ghost** *and with fire:*

John Baptizes Jesus

Descends back to Adam

And it came to pass in those days, when all the people were being baptizes by John in the Jordan. Jesus also came from Nazareth of Galilee, to be baptized.

But John forbad him, saying, *I have need to be baptized of thee, and comest thou to me?*

And Jesus answering said unto him, **Suffer it to be so now: for thus it becometh us to fulfil all righteousness.** Then he suffered him. And straightway coming up out of the water, Praying: he saw the heavens opened, and the *Holy Spirit* in bodily form descended liken as of a dove and lighten upon Him:

And there came a voice from heaven, saying, *Thou art my beloved Son, in whom I am well pleased.*

Jesus himself began to be about thirty years of age, being (as was supposed) the son of Joseph, which was the son of Heli, Which was the son of Matthat, which was the son of Levi, which was the son of Melchi, which was the son of Janna, which was the son of Joseph, Which was the son of Mattathias, which was the son of Amos, which was the son of Naum, which was the son of Esli, which was the son of Nagge, Which was the son of Maath, which was the son of Mattathias, which was the son of Semei, which was the son of Judah, which was the son of Joanna, which was the son of Zorobabel, which was the Salathiel, which was the son of Neri,

Which was the son of Melchi, which was the son of Addi, which was the son of Cosam, which was the son of Elmodam, which was the son of Er, Which was the son of Jose, which was the son of Eliezer, which was the son of Jorim, which was the son of Matthat, which was the son of Levi, Which was the son of Simeon, which was the son of Juda, which was the son of Joseph, which was the son of Jonan, which was the son of Eliakim, Which was the son of Melea, which was the son Menan which was the son of Mattatha, which was the son of Nathan, which was the son of David, Which was the son of Jesse, which was the son of Obed, which was the son of Booz, which was the son of Salmon, which was the son of Naasson, which was the son of Aminadab, which was the son of Aram, which was the son of Esrom, which was the son of Phares, which was the son of Juda, which was the son of Jacob, which was the son of Isaac, which was the son of Abraham, which was the son of Thara, which was the son of Nachor, Which was the son of Saruch, which was the son or Ragau, which was the son of Phalec, which was the son of Heber, which was the son of Sala, Which was the son of Cainan, which was the son of Arphaxad, which was the son to Sem, which was the son of Noah, which was the son of Lamech, Which was the son of Mathusala, which was the son of Enoch, which was the son of Jared, which was the son of Maleleel, which was the son of Cainan, Which was the son of Enos, which was the son of Seth, which was the son of Adam, which was the son of God.

Temptations in the Wilderness

Jesus being full of the *Holy Ghost* returned from Jordan, and was led by the Spirit into the wilderness. And when he had fasted forty days and forty nights, he was afterward an hungered. Then came the tempter Satan, unto him. Saying, If thou be the Son of God, command that these stones be made bread. But he answered and said, **It is written, Man shall not live by bread alone, but by every word that proceedeth out of the mouth of God**. Then the devil taketh him up into the holy city, Jerusalem, and setteth him on a pinnacle of the temple, And saith unto him, if thou be the Son of God, cast thyself down: for it is written, He shall give his angles charge concerning thee: and in their hands they shall bear thee up, lest at any time thou dash thy foot against a stone. Jesus said unto him, **It is written again, Thou shalt not tempt the Lord thy God.**

Again, the devil taketh him up into and exceeding high mountain, and showeth him all the kingdoms of the world, and the glory of them: in a moment of time, And saith unto him, all these things will I give thee, if thou wilt fall down and worship me. For all this power will I give thee, and the glory of them: for it has been delivered unto me: and to whomsoever I will give. If thou therefore wilt fall down and worship me, all shall be thine. Then saith Jesus unto him, **Get thee hence, Satan: for it is written, Thou shalt worship the Lord thy God, and him only shalt Ye serve, and worship.** Then the devil ended all the temptation, he departed from him for a season, and, behold, angels came and administered unto him.

John Proclaims Jesus the Messiah

The next day John seeth Jesus coming unto him, and saith, *Behold the lamb of God, which taketh away the sin of the world. This is he of whom I said, After me cometh a man which is preferred before me: for he was before me. And I knew him not: but that he should be made manifest to Israel, therefore am I come baptizing with water. And John bare record, saying, I saw the Spirit descending from heaven like a dove, and it abode upon him. And I knew him not: but he that sent me to baptize with water, the same said unto me, Upon whom thou shalt see the Spirit descending, and remaining on him, the same is he which baptizeth with the* **Holy Ghost**. *And I saw, and bare record that this is the Son of God.*

JESUS'S FIRST DISCIPLES

Again the next day after John stood, and two of his disciples; And looking upon Jesus as he walked, he saith, *Behold the Lamb of God!* And the two disciples heard him speak, and they followed Jesus. Then Jesus turned, and saw them following, and saith unto them, **What seek ye?** They said unto him, Rabbi, (which is to say, being interpreted, Master,) where dwellest thou? He saith unto them, **Come and see.** They came and saw where he dwelt, and abode with him that day: for it was about the tenth hour.

And one of the two which heard John speak, followed him, was Andrew, Simon Peter's brother. He first findeth his own brother Simon, and saith unto him, We have found the Messias, which is, being interpreted, the Christ. And he brought him to Jesus. And when Jesus beheld him, he said, **Thou art Simon the son of Jona: thou shalt be called Cephas, which is by interpretation, a stone.**

The day following Jesus would go forth into Galilee, and findeth Philip, and saith unto him, **Follow me.** Now Philip was of Bethsaida, the city of Andrew and Peter. Philip findeth Nathanael, and saith unto him, we have found him, of whom Moses in the law, and the prophets, did write, Jesus of *Nazareth, the son of Joseph.*

And Nathanael said unto him, Can there any good thing come out of Nazareth? Philip said unto him, Come and see. Jesus saw Nathanael coming to him, and said of him, **Behold an Israelite indeed, in whom is no guile!** Nathanael said unto him, whence knowest thou me? Jesus answered and said unto him.

Before that Philip called thee, when thou wast under the fig tree, I saw thee. Nathanael answered and said unto him, Rabbi, thou art the Son of God; thou art the King of Israel. Jesus answered and said unto him, **Because I said unto thee, I saw thee under the fig tree, believest thou? thou shalt see greater things than these.** And he saith unto him, **Verily, verily, I say unto you, Here after ye shall see heaven open, and the angels of God ascending and descending upon the Son of man.**

Water into Wine

And the third day there was a marriage in Cana of Galilee; and the mother of Jesus was there: And both Jesus was called, and his disciples, to the marriage. When they wanted wine, the mother of Jesus said unto him, They have no wine. Jesus saith unto her, **Woman, what have I to do with thee? mine hour is not yet come.** His mother said unto the servants, Whatsoever he saith unto you, do *it*. And there were set there six water pots of stone, after the manner of the purifying of the Jews, containing two or three firkins apiece. Jesus said unto them, **Fill the water pots with water.** And they filled them up to the brim. And he saith unto them, **Draw out now, and bear unto the governor of the feast.** And they bare *it*. When the ruler of the feast had tasted the water that was made wine, and knew not whence it was: (but the servants which drew the water knew;) the governor of the feast called the bridegroom, and saith unto him, Every man at the beginning doth set forth good wine; and when men have well drunk, then that which is worse: but thou hast kept the good wine until now. This beginning of miracles did Jesus in Cana of Galilee, and knew not whence it was and manifested forth his glory; and his disciples believed on him.

Ministry of Jesus Christ Clears the Temple

After this he went down to Capernaum, he, and his mother, and his brethren, and his disciples: and they continued there not many days. And the Jews' passover was at hand, and Jesus went up to Jerusalem, and found in the temple those that sold oxen and sheep and doves, and the changers of money sitting: And when he had made a scourge of small cords, he drove them all out of the temple, and the sheep, and the oxen; and poured out the changers' money, and overthrew the tables; And said unto them that sold doves, **Take these things hence; make not my Father's house an house of merchandise**. And his disciples remembered that it was written, *The zeal of thine house hath eaten me up.* Then answered the Jews and said unto him, What sign showest thou unto us, seeing that thou doest these things? Jesus answered and said unto them, **Destroy this temple, and in three days I will raise it up.** Then said the Jews, Forty and six years was this temple in building, and wilt thou rear it up in three days? But he spake of the temple of his body.

When therefore he was risen from the dead, his disciples remembered that he had said this unto them; and they believed the scripture, and the word which Jesus had said. Now when he was in Jerusalem at the passover, in the feast day, many believed in his name, when they saw the miracles which he did. But Jesus did not commit himself unto them, because he knew all men. And needed not that any should testify of man: for he knew what was in man. (but the servants which drew the water knew;)

Nicodemus Visits Jesus

There was a man of the Pharisees, named Nicodemus, a ruler of the Jews. The same came to Jesus by night, and said unto him, Rabbi, we know that thou art a teacher come from God: for no man can do these miracles that thou doest, except God be with him. Jesus answered and said unto him, **Verily, verily, I say unto thee, Except a man be born again, he cannot see the kingdom of God.** Nicodemus saith unto him, How can a man be born when he is old? Can he enter the second time into his mother's womb, and be born? Jesus answered, **Verily, verily, I say unto thee, Except a man be born of water and of the Spirit, he cannot enter into the kingdom of God. That which is born of the flesh is flesh; and that which is born of the Spirit is spirit. Marvel not that I said unto thee, Ye must be born again. The wind bloweth where it listeth, and thou hearest the sound thereof, but canst not tell whence it cometh, and whither it goeth: so is every one that is born of the Spirit.** Nicodemus answered and said unto him, How can these things be?

Jesus answered and said unto him, **Art thou a master of Israel, and knowest not these things? Verily, verily, I say unto thee, We speak that we do know, and testify that we have seen; and ye receive not our witness. If I have told you earthly things, and ye believe not, how shall ye believe, if I tell you of heavenly things?**

And no man hath ascended up to heaven, but he that came down from heaven, even the Son of man which is in heaven. And as Moses lifted up the serpent in the wilderness, even so must the Son of man be lifted up: That whosoever believeth in him should not

perish, but have eternal life. For God so loved the world, that he gave his only begotten Son, that whosoever believeth in him should not perish, but have everlasting life. For God sent not his Son into the world to condemn the world; but that the world through him might be saved. He that believeth on him is not condemned: but he that believeth not is condemned already, because he hath not believed in the name of the only begotten Son of God. And this is the condemnation, that light is come into the world, and men loved darkness rather than light, because their deeds were evil. For every one that doeth evil hateth the light, neither cometh to the light, lest his deeds should be reproved. But he that doeth truth cometh to the light, that his deeds may be made manifest, that they are wrought in God.

John the Baptist,
Tells more about Jesus

After these things came Jesus and his disciples into the land of Judaea; and there he tarried with them, and baptized. And John also was baptizing in Aenon near to Salim, because there was much water there: and they came, and were baptized. (For John was not yet cast into prison.) Then there arose a question between some of John's disciples and the Jews about purifying. And they came unto John, and said unto him, Rabbi, he that was with thee beyond Jordan, to whom thou barest witness, behold, the same baptizeth, and all men come to him.

John answered and said, *A man can receive nothing, except it be given him from heaven. Ye yourselves bear me witness, that I said, I am not the Christ, but that I am sent before him. He that hath the bride is the bridegroom: but the friend of the bridegroom, which standeth and heareth him, rejoiceth greatly because of the bride grooms voice: this my joy therefore is fulfilled. He must increase, but I must decrease.*

He that cometh from above is above all: he that is of the earth is earthly, and speaketh of the earth: he that cometh from heaven is above all. And what he hath seen and heard, that he testifieth; and no man receiveth his testimony. He that hath received his testimony hath set to seal that God is true. For he whom God hath sent speaketh the words of God: For God giveth not the Spirit by measure unto him. The Father loveth the Son, and hath given all things into his hand. He that believeth on the Son hath everlasting life: and he that believeth not the Son shall not see life; but the wrath of God abideth on him.

HEROD PUTS JOHN IN PRISON

And many other things in his exhortation preached he unto the people. But Herod the tetrarch, being reproved by him for Herodias his brother Philip's wife, and for all the evils which Herod had done, added yet this above all, that he shut up John in prison.

WOMAN AT THE WELL

When therefore the Lord knew how the Pharisees had heard that Jesus made and baptized more disciples than John, (Though Jesus himself baptized not, but his disciples,) He left Judaea, and departed again into Galilee. And he must needs go through Samaria. Then cometh he to a city of Samaria, which is called Sychar, near to the parcel of ground that Jacob gave to his son Joseph. Now Jacob's well was there.

Jesus therefore, being wearied with his journey, sat thus on the well: and it was about the sixth hour. There cometh a woman of Samaria to draw water: Jesus saith unto her, **Give me to drink.** (For his disciples were gone away unto the city to buy meat.) Then saith the woman of Samaria unto him, How is it that thou, being a Jew, askest drink of me, which am a woman of Samaria? for the Jews have no dealings with the Samaritans. Jesus answered and said unto her, **If thou knewest the gift of God, and who it is that saith to thee, Give me to drink; thou wouldest have asked of him, and he would have given thee living water**. The woman saith unto him, Sir, thou hast nothing to draw with, and the well is deep: from whence then hast thou that living water?

Art thou greater than our father Jacob, which gave us the well, and drank thereof himself, and his children, and his cattle? Jesus answered and said unto her, **Whosoever drinketh of this water shall thirst again: But whosoever drinketh of the water that I shall give him shall never thirst; but the water that I shall give him shall be in him a well of water springing up into everlasting life**. The woman saith unto him, Sir, give me this water, that I thirst not, neither come hither to draw. Jesus saith unto her, **Go, call thy husband, and come hither.** The woman answered and said, I have no husband. Jesus said unto her, **Thou hast well said, I have no husband: For thou hast had five husbands; and he whom thou now hast is not thy husband: in that say thou truly**.

The woman saith unto him, Sir, I perceive that thou art a prophet. Our fathers worshipped in this mountain; and ye say, that in Jerusalem is the place where men ought to worship. Jesus saith unto her, **Woman, believe me, the hour cometh, when ye shall neither in this mountain, nor yet at Jerusalem, worship the Father. Ye worship ye know not what: we know what we worship: for salvation is of the Jews. But the hour cometh, and now is, when the true worshippers shall worship the Father in spirit and in truth: for the Father seeketh such to worship him. God is a Spirit: and they that worship him must worship him in spirit and in truth.** The woman saith unto him, I know that Massiah cometh, which is called Christ: when he is come, he will tell us all things. Jesus saith unto her, **I that speak unto thee am he.**

Jesus tells of the Spiritual Harvest

And upon this came his disciples, and marvelled that he talked with the woman: yet no man said, What seekest thou? or, Why talkest thou with her? The woman then left her waterpot, and went her way into the city, and saith to the men, Come, see a man, which told me all things that ever I did: is not this the Christ? Then they went out of the city, and came unto him. In the mean while his disciples prayed him, saying, Master, eat. But he said unto them, **I have meat to eat that ye know** not of. Therefore said the disciples one to another, Hath any man brought him ought to eat? Jesus saith unto them, **My meat is to do the will of him that sent me, and to finish his work. Say not ye, There are yet four months, and then cometh harvest? behold, I say unto you, Lift up your eyes, and look on the fields; for they are white already to harvest. And he that reapeth receiveth wages, and gathereth fruit unto life eternal: that both he that soweth and he that reapeth may rejoice together. And herein is that saying true, One soweth, and another reapeth. I sent you to reap that whereon ye bestowed no labor: other men labored, and ye are entered into their labors.**

Many Samaritans Believe in Jesus

And many of the Samaritans of that city believed on him for the saying of the woman, which testified, He told me all that ever I did. So when the Samaritans were come unto him, they besought him that he would tarry with them: and he abode there two days. And many more believed because of his own word; and said unto the woman, Now we believe, not because of thy saying: for we have heard him ourselves, and know that this is indeed the Christ, the "Saviour" of the world.

Jesus Preaches in Galilee

Then Jesus had heard that John was cast into prison; after two days he departed leaving Nazareth, For Jesus himself testified, that a prophet hath no honor in his own country.

He came and dwelt in Capernaum, which is upon the sea coast, in the borders of Zabulon, and the land of Nephthalim, by the way of sea, beyond the Jordan, Galilee of the Gentiles; That it might be fulfilled which was spoken by Esaias the prophet. Saying! *The people which sat in darkness saw a great light; and to them which sat in region and shadow of death light is sprung up.*

And upon his return in power of the ***Holy Spirit:*** there went out a fame of him through all the region round about. And he taught in their synagogues, saying **The time is fulfilled, and the kingdom of God is at hand: repent ye, and believe the gospel.** Being glorified of all; the Galileans received him, having seen all the things that he did at Jerusalem and at the feast, for they also went unto the feast.

Jesus Heals a Government Official's Son

So Jesus came again into Cana of Galilee, where he made the water wine. And there was a certain nobleman, whose son was sick at Capernaum. When he heard that Jesus was come out of Judaea into Galilee, he went unto him, and besought him that he would come down, and heal his son: for he was at the point of death. Then said Jesus unto him, **Except ye see signs and wonders, ye will not believe.** The nobleman saith unto him, Sir, come down here my child die. Jesus saith unto him, **Go thy way; thy son liveth.** And the man believed the word that Jesus had spoken unto him, and he went his way. And as he was now going down, his servants met him, and told him, saying, Thy son liveth. Then enquired he of them the hour when he began to amend. And they said unto him, Yesterday at the seventh hour the fever left him. So the father knew that it was at the same hour, in the which Jesus said unto him, **Thy son liveth**: and himself believed, and his whole house.

Jesus is Rejected at Nazareth

And he came to Nazareth, where he had been brought up: and, as his custom was, he went into the synagogue on the sabbath day, and stood up for to read. And there was delivered unto him the book of the prophet Esaias. And when he had opened the book, he found the place where it was written, *The Spirit of the Lord is upon me, because he hath anointed me to preach the gospel to the poor; he hath sent me to heal the brokenhearted, to preach deliverance to the captives, and recovering of sight to the blind, to set at liberty them that are bruised, To preach the acceptable year of the Lord.* And he closed the book, and he gave *it* again to the minister, and sat down.

And the eyes of all them that were in the synagogue were fastened on him. And he began to say unto them, **This day is this scripture fulfilled in your ears**. And all bare him witness, and wondered at the gracious words which proceeded out of his mouth. And they said, Is not this Joseph's son?

And he said unto them, **Ye will surely say unto me this proverb, Physician, heal thyself: whatsoever we have heard done in Capernaum, do also here in thy country. And he said, Verily I say unto you, No prophet is accepted in his own country.**

But I tell you of a truth, many widows were in Israel in the days of Elias, when the heaven was shut up three years and six months, when great famine was throughout all the land; But unto none of them was Elias sent, save unto Sarepta, a city of Sidon, unto a woman that was a widow. And many lepers were in Israel in the time of Eliseus the prophet; and none of them was cleansed, saving

Naaman the Syrian. And all they in the synagogue, when they heard these things, were filled with wrath, and rose up, and thrust him out of the city, and led him unto the brow of the hill whereon their city was built, that they might cast him down headlong. But he passing through the midst of them went his way.

Four Fishermen Called by Jesus

Now as he walked by the sea of Galilee, he saw two brethren, Simon called *Peter,* and *Andrew* casting their net into the sea: for they were fishers. And Jesus said unto them, **Come Follow me, and I will make you fishers of men.** And they straightway left their nets, and followed him. And when he had gone a little further thence, he saw *James* the son of Zebedee, and *John* his brother, in a ship mending their nets. And straightway he called them: and they left their father Zebedee in the ship with the hired servants, and went after him.

Jesus Teaches with Great Authority

And they went into Capernaum; a city of Galilee, straightway on the sabbath day he entered into the synagogue and taught. And the people were amazed at his teaching, because he taught them as one who had authority, not as the teachers of the law. And there was in their synagogue a man possessed with an unclean spirit; a devil. Saying, at the top of his voice, Let us alone; what have we to do with thee, thou Jesus of Nazareth? Art thou come to destroy us? I know thee who thou art; *The Holy One of God.* Jesus rebuked him, saying, **Hold thy peace, and come out of him,** And then the devil had shook him valiantly, he threw him down in the midst, and he came out of him, with a loud cry, and hurt him not, and they were all amazed, insomuch that they questioned among themselves, saying, What thing is this? what new doctrine is this? for with authority and power commandeth he even the unclean spirits, and they do obey him and come out. And immediately his fame spread abroad throughout all the region in every place, about the country.

Jesus Heals Peter's Mother-in-law and Many Others

And forthwith, when they were come out of the synagogue, they entered into the house of Simon Peter and Andrew, with James and John. And Simon's mother-in-law was taken with a great fever; and they besought him for her. And he stood over her, and rebuked the fever. And he came and took her by the hand, and lifted her up; and immediately the fever left her, and she arose, and ministered unto them.

And at even, when the sun was setting, all they that had any sickness with divers diseases and them that were possessed with devils, gathered together at the door. And with the laying on of hands and at his word he healed many that were sick and diseased, and cast out many devils; that cried out saying, ***Thou art Christ the Son of God.*** And he suffered them not to speak, because they knew him. That it might be fulfilled which was spoken by Esaias the prophet, saying, *He Himself took our infirmities, and bare our sicknesses.*

Jesus Preaches throughout Galilee

And in the morning, rising up a great while before day, he went out, and departed into a solitary place, and there prayed. And Simon and they that were with him followed after him, and when they found Him, they said unto him, all the people seek thee, and have come beseeching that ye should not depart from them. **And he said unto them, I must preach the kingdom of God to other cities also: for therefore am I sent.**

And Jesus went about all Galilee, teaching in their synagogues, and preaching the gospel of the kingdom, and healing all manner of sickness and all manner of disease among the people.

And his fame went throughout all Syria: and they brought unto him all sick people with divers diseases and torments, and those which were possessed with devils, and those which were lunatic, and those that had the palsy; and he healed them, and there followed him great multitudes of people from Galilee, Decapolis, Jerusalem, Judaea, and from beyond Jordan.

Miraculous Catch of Fish

And it came to pass, that, as the people pressed upon him to hear the word of God, he stood by the lake of Gennesaret, and saw two ships by the lake shore, but the fishermen were gone out of them, and were washing their nets. And he entered into one of the ships, which was Simon's, and prayed him that he would thrust out a little from the land. And he sat down, and taught the people out of the ship.

Now when he had left speaking, he said unto Simon, **Launch out into the deep, and let down your nets for a draught.** And Simon answering said unto him, Master, we have toiled all the night, and have taken nothing: nevertheless at thy word I will let down the net. And when they had this done, they in closed a great multitude of fishes: and their net began to brake. And they beckoned unto their partners, which were in the other ship, that they should come and help them. And they came, and filled both the ships, so that they began to sink.

When Simon Peter saw *it,* he fell down at Jesus' knees, saying, depart from me; for I am a sinful man, O Lord. For he was astonished, and all that were with him, at the draught of the fishes which they had taken: And so was also James, and John, the sons of Zebedee, which were partners with Simon. And Jesus said unto Simon, **Fear not; from henceforth thou shalt catch men.** And when they had brought their ships to land, they forsook all, and followed him.

Then went he up onto a high mountain pray.

Jesus Heals Man with Leprosy

When he was come down from the mountain, he came into a certain city, and great multitude followed him. And there came a leper, and seeing Jesus, knelt down with his face to the ground, and worshiped him saying, Lord, if thou wilt, thou canst make me clean. And Jesus was moved with compassion, put forth his hand, and touched him, **saying, I will: be thou clean**. And immediately his leprosy departed from him and he was cleansed. **And Jesus saith unto him, See thou tell no man; but go thy way, show thyself to the priest, and offer the gift. Moses commanded, for a testimony unto them.** But he went out, and began to publish it much, blazing the matter abroad: insomuch that Jesus could no more openly enter into the city, but great multitudes came together coming from ever quarter to hear, and to be healed by him of their infirmities, and straightway after He healed them, charged them fort with and sent them away. And he withdrew himself into the wilderness, to pray.

Jesus Heals a Paralyzed Man

And he entered into a ship, and passed over, and came into his own city. Capernaum; and it was noised that he was in the house. It came to pass on a certain day, as he was teaching, that there were Pharisees and doctors of the law sitting by, which were come out of every town of Galilee, and Judaea, and Jerusalem: and the power of Lord was present to heal many who were sick, So many gathered together, insomuch that there was no room to receive them, not so much as about the door; and he preached the word unto them. And behold, They came unto him, bringing one sick of the palsy; which was borne of four. And when they could not come nigh unto him for the press, they uncovered the roof where he was: and when they had broken it up, they let down the bed wherein the sick of the palsy lay. Into their midst, before Jesus. When Jesus saw their faith, he said unto the sick of the palsy, **Son, be of good cheer; thy sins be forgiven thee**.

But there were certain of the scribes sitting there, and reasoning in their hearts, Who is this which speaketh blasphemies? Who can forgive sins but God only? And immediately when Jesus perceived in his spirit that they so reasoned within themselves, he said unto them, **Wherefore think ye evil in your hearts? Whether is it easier to say to the sick of the palsy, Thy sins be forgiven thee; or to say, Arise, and take up thy bed, and walk? But that ye may know that the Son of man hath power on earth to forgive sins, (He saith to the sick of the palsy,) I say unto thee, Arise, and take up thy bed, and go thy way into thine house.** And immediately he rose up before them, and took up that whereon he lay, and departed to his own house, glorifying God. And they were all amazed, and they glorified God, and were filled with fear, saying, We have seen marvelous things this day.

JESUS EATS WITH SINNERS

And he went forth again by the sea side; and all the multitude resorted unto him, and he taught them. And as he passed by, he saw Levi, a publican tax collector, son of Alphaeus Matthew by name sitting at the receipt of custom, and said unto Him, **Follow me.** And he left all, rose up, and followed him. It came to pass, Matthew, made Jesus a great feast in his own house: And many publicans and sinners sat also together with Jesus and his disciples: for there were many, and they followed him. And when the scribes and Pharisees saw him eat with publicans and sinners, they said unto his disciples, Why eateth your Master with publicans and sinners? But when Jesus heard that which, he said unto them, **They that be whole need not a physician, but they that are sick. But go ye and learn what that meaneth, I will have mercy, and not sacrifice: for I am not come to call the righteous, but sinners to repentance.**

Ask Jesus about Fasting

Then came to him the disciples of John, saying, Why do we and the Pharisees fast oft, and make prayers, but thine eat and drink and fast not?

And Jesus said unto them, **Can the children of the bridechamber fast and mourn, as long as the bridegroom is with them? But when the bridegroom shall be taken away from them, and then shall they fast in those days.** And he spake also a parable unto them, **No man also seweth a piece of new cloth on an old garment: else the new piece, for that which is put in to fill it up taketh from the garment, and the rent is made worse.**

Neither do men put new wine into old bottles; else the new wine will burst the bottles, and be spilled, and the bottles shall perish. But new wine must be put into new bottles; and both are preserved. No man also having drunk old wine straightway desireth new: for he saith, The old is better.

Jesus Heals a Lame Man by the Pool

After this there was a feast of the Jews; and Jesus went up to Jerusalem. Now there is at Jerusalem by the sheep market a pool, which is called in the Hebrew tongue Bethesda, having five porches. In these lay a great multitude of impotent folk, of blind, halt, and withered, waiting for the moving of the water. For an angel went down at a certain season into the pool, and troubled the water: whosoever then first after the troubling of the water stepped in was made whole of whatsoever disease he had.

And a certain man was there, which had an infirmity thirty and eight years. When Jesus saw him lie, and knew that he had been now a long time in that case, he saith unto him, **Wilt thou be made whole?** The impotent man answered him, Sir, I have no man, when the water is troubled, to put me into the pool: but while I am coming, another steppeth down before me. Jesus saith unto him, **Rise, take up thy bed, and walk.**

And immediately the man was made whole, and took up his bed, and walked: and on the same day was the sabbath. The Jews therefore said unto him that was cured, It is the sabbath day: it is not lawful for thee to carry thy bed. He answered them, He that made me whole, the same said unto me, Take up thy bed, and walk. Then asked they him, What man is that which said unto thee, Take up thy bed, and walk? And he that was healed knew not who it was: for Jesus had conveyed himself away, for multitude being in that place.

Afterward Jesus findeth him in the temple, and said unto him, **Behold, thou art made whole: sin no more, lest a worse thing come**

unto thee. The man departed, and told the Jews that it was Jesus, which had made him whole. And therefore did the Jews persecute Jesus, and sought to slay him, because he had done these things on the sabbath day. But Jesus answered them, **My Father worketh hitherto, and I work.**

Therefore the Jews sought the more to kill him, because he not only had broken the sabbath, but said also that God was his Father, making himself equal with God.

Then Answered Jesus Said unto Them

Verily, verily, I say unto you, The Son can do nothing of himself, but what he seeth the Father do: for what things soever he doeth, these also doeth the Son likewise. For the Father loveth the Son, and showeth him all things that himself doeth: and he will show him greater works than these, that ye may marvel. For as the Father raiseth up the dead, and quickeneth them; even so the Son quickeneth whom he will. For the Father judgeth no man, but hath committed all judgment unto the Son: That all men should honor the Son, even as they honor the Father. He that honoreth not the Son honoreth not the Father which hath sent him. Verily, verily, I say unto you, He that heareth my word, and believeth on him that sent me, hath everlasting life, and shall not come into condemnation; but is passed from death unto life. Verily, I say unto you, The hour is coming, and now is, when the dead shall hear the voice of the Son of God: and they that hear shall live. For as the Father hath life in himself; so hath he given to the Son to have life in himself; And hath given him authority to execute judgment also, because he is the Son of man. Marvel not at this: for the hour is coming, in the which all that are in the graves shall hear his voice, And shall come forth; they that have done good, unto the resurrection of life; and they that have done evil, unto the resurrection of damnation. I can of mine own self do nothing: as I hear, I judge: and my judgment is just; because I seek not mine own will, but the will of the Father which hath sent me.

Jesus Supports His Claim

If I bear witness of myself, my witness is not true. There is another that bareth witness of me; and I know that the witness which he witnesseth of me is true. He sent unto John, and he bare witness unto the truth. But I receive not testimony from man: but these things I say, that ye might be saved. He was a burning and a shining light: and ye were willing for a season to rejoice in his light. But I have greater witness than that of John: for the works which the Father hath given me to finish, the same works that I do, bear witness of me, that the Father hath sent me. And the Father himself, which hath sent me, hath borne witness of me. Ye have neither heard his voice at any time, nor seen his shape. And ye have not his word abiding in you: for whom he hath sent, him ye believe not. You Search the scriptures; for in them ye think ye have eternal life and they are they which testify of me.

And ye will not come to me, that ye might have life. I receive not honor from men. But I know you, that ye have not the love of God in you. I am come in my Father's name, and ye receive me not: if another shall come in his own name, him ye will receive. How can ye believe, which receive honor one of another, and seek not the honor that cometh from God only? Do not think that I will accuse you to the Father: there is one that accuseth you, even Moses, in whom ye trust. For had ye believed Moses, ye would have believed me: for he wrote of me. But if ye believe not his writings, how shall ye believe my words?

Picking Corn on the Sabbath

And it came to pass, at that time on the second sabbath after the first, that Jesus when he was hungered and his disciples that were with him went through the corn fields on the sabbath day; and began to pluck the ears of corn, rubbing them in their hands and began to eat. And certain of the Pharisees saw it they said unto him, Behold, why do ye and thy disciples do that which is not lawful to do upon the sabbath day? But Jesus answering them said, **Have ye not read so much as this, what David did, when he was hungered, and they that were with him; How he entered into the house of God in the days of Abiathar the high priest, and did eat the showbread, which is not lawful to eat but for the priests, and gave also to them which were with him? Or have ye not read in the law, how that on the sabbath days the priests in the temple profane the sabbath, and are blameless? But I say unto you, that in this place is one greater than the temple. But if ye had known what this meaneth, I will have mercy, and not sacrifice, ye would not have condemned the guiltless. The sabbath was made for man, and not man for the sabbath: For the Son of man is Lord even of the sabbath day.**

Jesus Heals on the Sabbath

And when he was departed thence, and on another sabbath, he entered into the synagogue and taught: and there was a man whose right hand was withered. And the scribes and Pharisees watched him, whether he would heal on the sabbath day; that they might find an accusation against him. Then they asked him, saying, Is it lawful to heal on the sabbath days? So he said unto them, **What man shall there be among you, that haveth one sheep, and if it fall into a pit on the sabbath day, will he not lay hold it, and lift it out? How much then is a man better than a sheep? Wherefore it is lawful to do well on the sabbath days. But he knewth their thoughts, as they held their peace.** And when he had looked round about on them with anger, being grieved for the hardness of their hearts, he saith unto the man, **Rise up and stand forth in the midst.** And he arose and stood forth. Then said Jesus unto them, **I will ask you one thing; Is it lawful on the sabbath days to do good. Or to do evil? To save life, or to destroy it?** Then said he unto the man with the withered and hand **Stretch forth thy hand.** And he did so: and his hand was restored whole, like as the other. And they were filled with madness; and the Pharisees went forth, and communed one with another what they might do to Jesus. And how they might destroy him.

Large crowds follow Jesus

But when Jesus knew it, he withdrew himself from thence: with his disciples to the sea: and a great multitude from Galilee followed him, and from Judaea, and healed them all; And said unto them **speak not of this to no one. That it might be fulfilled which was spoken by Esaias the prophet, saying,** *Behold my servant, whom I have chosen; my beloved, in whom my soul is well pleased: I will put spirit upon him, and he shall show judgment unto the Gentiles. He shall not strive, nor cry; neither shall and man hear his voice in the streets. A bruised reed shall he not break, and smoking flax shall he not quench, till he send forth judgment unto victory. And his name shall the Gentiles trust.* Also they came from Jerusalem, and from Idumaea, and from beyond the jordan; and they about Tyre and Sidon, a great multitude, when they had heard what great things he did came unto him. And he spake unto his disciples, that a small ship should wait on him because of the multitude lest they should throng him. For he had healed many; insomuch that they pressed upon him for to thouch him, as many as had plagues. And unclean spirits, when they saw him, fell down before him, and cried, saying. Thou art the Son of God. And he straitly charged them that they should not make him known.

Jesus Selects the Twelve Disciples

And it came to pass in those days, that he went out into a mountain to pray, and continued all night in prayer to God his Farther.

When it was day, he called unto him his disciples; whom he ordained: and of them he would chose twelve, whom he also named apostles; that they should be with him, and that he might send them forth to preach. And to have power to heal sicknesses, and cast out devils: Simon he surnamed *Peter;* and *James* the son of Zebedee, and *John* the brother of *James:* and he surnamed them Boanerges, which is, The sons of thunder: And *Andrew, and Philip, and Bartholomew, and Matthew, and Thomas,* and *James* the son of Alphaeus; and *Thaddaeus,* and *Simon* the Canaanite, and *Judas* Iscariot, which also betrayed him: and they went into an house.

Jesus Gives the Beatitudes

And seeing the multitudes, he went up into a mountain: and when he sat, his disciples came unto him: and he taught them, as they sat down with him: then he stood up in the company of his disciples, and a great multitude of people came out of Judaea and Jerusalem, and from the sea cost of Tyre and Sidon, which came to hear him, and to be healed of their diseases;

And they that were vexed with unclean spirits: And the whole multitude sought him: for there went virtue out of him, and healed them all.

Then said He, **Blessed are ye, when men shall hate you, and when they shall separate you from their company, and shall reproach you, and cast out your name as evil, for the Son of man's sake. Rejoice ye in that day, and leap for joy: being exceeding glad: for, behold, great is your reward in heaven: for in like manner did their fathers unto the prophets. But woe unto you that are full! For ye shall hunger. Woe unto you that laugh now! For ye shall mourn and weep. Woe unto you, when all men shall speak well of you! For so did their fathers to the false prophets.**

Blessed are the poor in spirit: for theirs is the kingdom of heaven. Blessed are they that mourn: for they shall be comforted. Blessed are the meek; for they shall inherit the earth. Blessed are they which do hunger and thirst after righteousness: for they shall be filled. Blessed are the merciful: for they shall obtain mercy. Blessed are the pure in heart: for they shall see God. Blessed are the peacemakers: for they shall be called the children of God. Blessed

are they which are persecuted for righteousness' sake: for theirs is the kingdom of heaven. Blessed are ye, when men shall revile you, and persecute you, and shall say all manner of evil against you falsely, for my sake. Rejoice, and be exceeding glad: for great is your reward in heaven: for so persecuted they the prophets which were before you.

Salt and Light

Ye are the salt of the earth: but if the salt have lost his savour, wherewith shall it be salted? It is thenceforth good for nothing, but to be cast out, and to be trodden under foot of men. Ye are the light of the world. A city that is set on an hill cannot be hid. Neither do men light a candle, and put it under a bushel, but on a candlestick; and it giveth light unto all that are in the house. Let your light so shine before men, that they may see your good works, and glorify your Father which is in heaven.

The Law

Think not that I am come to destroy the law, or the prophets: I am not come to destroy, but to fulfill. For verily I say unto you, till heaven and earth pass, not one jot or one tittle shall in no wise pass from the law, till all be fulfilled. Whosoever therefore shall break one of these least commandments, and shall teach men so, he shall be called the least in the kingdom of heaven: but whosoever shall do and teach them, the same shall be called great in the kingdom of heaven. For I say unto you, that except your righteousness shall exceed the righteousness of the scribes and Pharisees, ye shall in no case enter into the kingdom of heaven.

JESUS TEACHES ABOUT ANGER

Ye have heard that it was said by them of old time, Thou shalt not kill; and whosoever shall kill shall be in danger of the judgment: But I say unto you, That whosoever is angry with his brother without a cause shall be in danger of the judgment: and whosoever shall say to his brother, Raca, shall be in danger of the council: but whosoever shall say, Thou fool, shall be in danger of hell fire. Therefore if thou bring thy gift to the altar, and there rememberest that thy brother hath ought against thee; Leave there thy gift before the altar, and go thy way; first be reconciled to thy brother, and then come and offer thy gift. Agree with thine adversary quickly, whiles thou art in the way with him; lest at any time the adversary deliver ye to the judge, and the judge deliver thee to the officer, and thou be cast into prison. Verily I say unto thee, Thou shalt by no means come out thence, till thou hast paid the uttermost farthing.

About Lust

Ye have heard that it was said by them of old time, Thou shalt not commit adultery: But I say unto you, That whosoever looketh on a woman to lust after her hath committed adultery with her already in his heart. And if thy right eye offend thee, pluck it out, and cast it from thee: for it is profitable for thee that one of thy members should perish, and not that thy whole body should be cast into hell. And if thy right hand offend thee, cut it off, and cast it from thee: for it is profitable for thee that one of thy members should perish, and not that thy whole body should be cast into hell.

Teaches about Divorce

It hath been said, Whosoever shall put away his wife, let him give her a writing of divorcement: But I say unto you, That whosoever shall put away his wife, saving for the cause of fornication, causeth her to commit adultery: and whosoever shall marry her that is divorced committeth adultery. Again, ye have heard that it hath been said by them of old time.

ABOUT VOWS

Thou shalt not forswear thyself, but shalt perform unto the Lord thine oaths: But I say unto you, Swear not at all; neither by heaven; for it is God's throne: Nor by the earth; for it is his footstool: neither by Jerusalem; for it is the city of the great King. Neither shalt thou swear by thy head, because thou canst not make one hair white or black. But let your communication be, yea, yea; nay, nay: for whatsoever is more than these cometh of evil.

Jesus Teaches about Retaliation

Ye have heard that it hath been said, an eye for an eye, and a tooth for a tooth: But I say unto you, that ye resist not evil: but whosoever shall smite thee on thy right cheek, turn to him the other also.

And if any man will sue thee at the law, and take away thy coat, let him have thy cloak also. And whosoever shall compel thee to go a mile, go with him twain. Give to him that asketh thee, and from him that would borrow of thee turn not thou away.

Jesus Teaches about Loving Enemies

Ye have heard that it hath been said; Thou shalt love thy neighbor, and hate thine enemy. But I say unto you, Love your enemies, bless them that cruise you, do good to them that hate you, and pray for them which despitefully use you, and persecute you; Give to every man that asketh of thee; and of him that taketh away thy goods ask them not again, And as ye would that men should do to you, do ye also to them likewise. For if ye do good to them which do good to you, what thank have ye? For sinners also do even the same. And if Ye lend to them of whom ye hope to receive, what thank have ye? For sinners also lend to sinners, to receive as much again. But again I say to you Love your enemies, bless them that curse you, do good to them that hate you; and lend hoping for nothing again; and your reward shall be great, and ye shall be the children of the father; for he is kind unto the unthankful and to the evil. For he maketh his sun to rise on the evil and on the good, and sendeth rain on the just and on the unjust. For if ye love them which love you, what reward have ye? Do not even the publicans the same? Be ye therefore perfect, even as your Father which is in heaven is perfect.

Teaches about Giving to the Needy

Take heed that ye do not your alms before men, to be seen of them: otherwise ye have no reward of your Father which is in heaven. Therefore when thou doest thine alms, do not sound a trumpet before thee, as the hypocrites do in the synagogues and in the streets, that they may have glory of men. Verily I say unto you, They have their reward. But when thou doest alms, let not thy left hand know what thy right hand doeth: That thine alms may be in secret: and thy Father which seeth in secret himself shall reward thee openly.

Jesus Teaches How to Pray

And when thou prayest, thou shalt not be as the hypocrites are: for they love to pray standing in the synagogues and in the corners of the streets, that they may be seen of men. Verily I say unto you, They have their reward. So when thou prayest, enter into thy closet, and when thou hast shut thy door, pray to thy Father which is in secret; and thy Father which seeth in secret shall reward thee openly. But when ye pray, use not vain repetitions, as the heathen do: for they think that they shall be heard for their much speaking. Be not ye therefore like unto them: for your Father knoweth what things ye have need of, before ye ask him. After this manner therefore pray ye: *Our Father which art in heaven, Hallowed be thy name. Thy kingdom come. Thy will be done in earth, as it is in heaven. Give us this day our daily bread. And forgive us our debts, as we forgive our debtors. And lead us not into temptation, but deliver us from evil: For thine is the kingdom, and the power, and the glory, for ever. Amen.* For if ye forgive men their trespasses, your heavenly Father will also forgive you: But if ye forgive not men their trespasses, neither will your Father forgive your trespasses.

Teaches about Fasting

Moreover when ye fast, be not, as the hypocrites, of a sad countenance: for they disfigure their faces that they may appear unto men to fast. Verily I say unto you, They have their just do. But thou, when thou fastest, anoint thine head, and wash thy face; That thou appear not unto men to fast, but unto thy Father which is in secret: and thy Father, which seeth in secret, shall reward thee openly.

About Money

Lay not up for yourselves treasures upon earth, where moth and rust doth corrupt, and where thieves break through and steal: But lay up for yourselves treasures in heaven, where neither moth nor rust doth corrupt, and where thieves do not break through nor steal: For where your treasure is, there will your heart be also.

The Light of the Body

The light of the body is the eye: if therefore thine eye be single, thy whole body shall be full of light. But if thine eye be evil, thy whole body shall be full of darkness. If therefore the light that is in thee be darkness, how great is that darkness! No man can serve two masters: for either he will hate the one, and love the other; or else he will hold to the one, and despise the other. Ye cannot serve God and mammon.

Worry

Therefore I say unto you, Take no thought for your life, what ye shall eat, or what ye shall drink; nor yet for your body, what ye shall put on. Is not the life more than meat, and the body then raiment? Behold the fowls of the air: for they sow not, neither do they reap, nor gather into barns; yet your heavenly Father feedeth them. Are ye not much better than they? Which of you by taking thought can add one cubit unto his stature? And why take ye thought for raiment? Consider the lilies of the field, how they grow; they toil not, neither do they spin: And yet I say unto you, That even Solomon in all his glory was not arrayed like one of these. Wherefore, if God so clothe the grass of the field, which today is, and tomorrow is cast into the oven, shall he not much more clothe you, O ye of little faith? Therefore take no thought, saying, what shall we eat? Or, Wherewithal shall we be clothed? (For after all these things do the Gentiles seek:) for your heavenly Father knoweth that ye have need of these things. But seek ye first the kingdom of God, and his righteousness; and all these things shall be added unto you. Take therefore no thought for the morrow: for the morrow shall take thought for the things of itself. Sufficient unto the day is the evil thereof.

Jesus Teaches
about Judging Others

Judge not, that ye shall not be judged: condemn not and ye shall not be condemned: for with what measure ye mete, it shall be measured to you again. Forgive; and ye shall be forgiven: Give and it shall be given unto you. And he spake a parable unto them, Can the blind lead the blind? Shall they not both fall into the ditch? The disciple is not above his master: but every one that is perfected shall be as his master. And why wilt thou say to thy brother, Let me pull out the mote out of thine eye; but perceivest not the beam that is in thine own eye? Thou hypocrite, first cast out the beam out of thine own eye; and then shalt thou see clearly to cast out the mote out of thy bother's eye. Give not that which is holy unto the dogs, neither cast ye your pearls before swine, lest they trample them under their feet, and turn again and rent you.

Asking, Seeking, Knocking

Ask, and it shall be given you; seek, and ye shall find; knock, and it shall be opened unto you: For every one that asketh receiveth; and he that seeketh findeth; and to him that knocketh it shall be opened. Or what man is there of you, whom if his son ask bread, will he give him a stone? Or if he ask a fish, will he give him a serpent? If ye then, being evil, know how to give good gifts unto your children, how much more shall your Father which is in heaven give good things to them that ask him? Therefore all things whatsoever ye would that men should do unto you, do ye even so unto them: for this is the law and the prophets.

Jesus the Way to Heaven

Enter ye in at the strait gate: for wide is the gate, and broad is the way, that leadeth to destruction, and many there be that which goth in there to: Because strait is the gate, and narrow is the way, which leadeth unto life, and few there be that find it.

Fruit in People's Lives

Beware of false prophets, which come to you in sheep's clothing, but inwardly they are ravening wolves. Ye shall know them by their fruits. Do men gather grapes from thorns, or figs of bramble bush? Even so every good tree bringeth forth good fruit; but a corrupt tree bringeth forth bad fruit. Every tree that bringeth not forth good fruit is hewn down, and cast into the fire. Wherefore by their fruits ye shall know them.

A good man out of the good treasure of his heart bringeth forth that which is good; and an evil man out evil treasure of his heart bringeth forth that which is evil: for of the abundance of the heart his mouth speaketh.

Building on a Solid Foundation

Why call ye me, Lord, Lord, and do not the things which I say? Not every one that saith unto me, Lord, Lord, shall enter into the kingdom of heaven; but he that doeth the will of my Father which is in heaven. Many will say to me in that day, Lord, Lord, have we not prophesied in thy name? And in thy name cast out devils? And in thy name done many wonderful works? And then will I profess unto them, I never knew you: depart from me, ye that work iniquity. Whosoever cometh to me, and heareth my sayings, and doeth them, I will liken him unto a wise man, which built his house upon a rock: and dug deep, the foundation. And the rain descended, and stream rose, the wind blew and the floods came, and beat vehemently upon that house but could not shake it:

But he that heareth, these sayings of mine, and doeth them not, shall be likened unto a foolish man, which built his house upon the sand without a foundation. And the rain descended, and the floods came, and the winds blew, and beat upon that house; and it fell: and great was the fall of it. And it came to pass, when Jesus had ended these sayings, the people were astonished at his doctrine: For he taught them as one having authority, and not as the scribes.

Roman Soldier Demonstrates Faith

And then he had ended all his sayings in the audience of the people. He entered into Capernaum. And there come unto Him a certain centurion, for he loveth the nation and hath built the people a synagogue, having heard of Jesus. He had a servant, who was dear unto him, how was sicken, and ready to die. Saying, Lord, my servant lieth at home sick of the palsy, grievously tormented, I beseech ye if you are willing heal my servant. Jesus said unto him, **I will come and heal him**;

The centurion answered and said, Lord, I am not worthy that thou shouldest come under my roof: but speak the word only, and my servant shall be healed. For I am a man under authority, having soldiers under me: and I say to this man, Go and he goeth: and to another, Come and he cometh; and to my servant, Do this, and he doeth it. When Jesus heard it, He marveled, and said to them that followed. **Verily I say unto you, I have not found so great faith, no, not in Israel. And I say unto you, That many shall come from the east and west, and shall sit down with Abraham, and Isaac, and Jacob, in the kingdom of heaven. But the children of the kingdom shall be cast out into outer darkness: where there shall be weeping and gnashing of teeth. And Jesus said unto the centurion, Go thy way; and as thou hast believed, so be it done unto thee.** And his servant was healed in the selfsame hour.

Widow's Son Is Raised from the Dead

And it came to pass the day after, that he went into a city called Nain; and many of his disciples went with him. Now when he came nigh to the gate of the city, behold, there was a dead man carried out, the only son of his mother, and she was a widow: and much people of the city was with her.

And when the Lord saw her, he had compassion on her, and said unto her, **Weep not.** And he came and touched the bier: and they that bare him stood still. And he said, **Young man, I say unto thee, Arise.** And he that was dead sat up, and began to speak. And Jesus delivered him to his mother. And there came a fear on all: and they glorified God, saying, That a great prophet is risen up among us; and, That God hath visited his people. And this rumor of him went forth throughout all Judaea, and throughout all the region round about.

JESUS EASES JOHN'S DOUBT

And it came to pass, when Jesus had made an end of commanding his twelve disciples, he departed thence to teach and to preach in their cities. Now when John, who was in the prison, heard of all the works of Christ. He called unto him two of his disciples and sent them to Jesus, saying, Art thou he that should come? Or do we look for another?

When the men were come unto him, they said, John the Baptist hath sent us unto thee, saying, Art thou he that should come? Or do we look for another? And in that same hour, he cured many of their infirmities and plagues, and of evil spirits; and unto many that were blind he gave sight, Then Jesus said unto them, **Go your way and show what things ye have seen and heard; how that the blind see, the lame walk, the lepers are cleansed, the deaf hear, the dead are raised, and have the gospel preached to them. And blessed is he, whosoever shall not be offended in me.**

What Jesus Said about John

And as they departed, Jesus began to say unto the multitudes concerning John, **What went ye out into the wilderness to see? A reed shaken with the wind? But what went ye out for to see? A man clothed in soft raiment? behold, they that wear soft clothing are in kings' houses. But what went ye out for to see? A prophet? yea, I say unto you, and more than a prophet. For this is he, of whom it is written,** *Behold, I send my messenger before thy face, which shall prepare thy way before thee.* **Verily I say unto you, Among them that are born of women there hath not risen a greater than John the Baptist: notwithstanding he that is least in the kingdom of heaven is greater than he. And from the days of John the Baptist until now the kingdom of heaven suffereth violence, and the violent take it by force. For all the prophets and the law prophesied until John. And if ye will receive it, this is Elias, which was for to come. He that hath ears to hear, let him hear. But whereunto shall I liken this generation? It is like unto children sitting in the markets, and calling unto their fellows, and saying, We have piped unto you, and ye have not danced; we have mourned unto you, and ye have not lamented. For John came neither eating nor drinking, and they say, He hath a devil. The Son of man came eating and drinking, and they say, Behold a man gluttonous, and a winebibber, a friend of publicans and sinners. But wisdom is justified of her children.**

Rest for the Soul

Then began he to denounce the cities wherein most of his mighty works were done, because they repented not: **Woe unto thee, Chorazin! woe unto thee, Bethsaida! for if the mighty works, which were done in you, had been done in Tyre and Sidon, they would have repented long ago in sackcloth and ashes. But I say unto you, it shall be more tolerable for Tyre and Sidon at the day of judgment, than for you.**

And thou, **Capernaum, which art exalted unto heaven, shalt be brought down to hell: for if the mighty works, which have been done in thee, had been done in Sodom, it would have remained until this day. But I say unto you, that it shall be more tolerable for the land of Sodom in the day of judgment, than for thee.**

At that time Jesus answered and said, **I thank thee, O Father, Lord of heaven and earth, because thou hast hid these things from the wise and prudent, and hast revealed them unto babes. Even so, Father: for so it seemed good in thy sight. All things are delivered unto me of my Father: and no man knoweth the Son, but the Father; neither knoweth any man the Father, save the Son, and he to whomsoever the Son will reveal him. Come unto me, all ye that labour and are heavy laden and I will give you rest. Take my yoke upon you, and learn of me; for I am meek and lowly in heart: and ye shall find rest unto your souls. For my yoke is easy, and my burden is light.**

Sinful Woman Anoints Jesus's Feet

And one of the Pharisees desired of him that he would eat with him. And he went in unto the Pharisee's house, and sat down to meat. And, behold, a woman in the city, which was a sinner, when she knew that Jesus sat at meat in the Pharisee's house, brought an alabaster box of ointment, and stood behind him at his feet, weeping, and began to wash his feet with her tears, and did wipe them with the hairs of her head, and kissed his feet, and anointed them with the ointment.

Now when the Pharisee which had bidden him saw it, he spake within himself, saying, This man, if he were a prophet, would have known who and what manner of woman this is that toucheth him: for she is a sinner. And Jesus answering said unto him, **Simon, I have somewhat to say unto thee.**

And he saith, Master, say on. **There was a certain creditor which had two debtors: the one owed five hundred pence, and the other fifty. And when they had nothing to pay, he frankly forgave them both. Tell me therefore, which of them will love him most?** Simon answered and said, I suppose that he, to whom he forgave most. And he said unto him, **Thou hast rightly judged. And he turned unto the woman, and said to Simon, Seest thou this woman? I entered into thine house, thou gavest me no water for my feet: but she hath washed my feet with tears, and wiped them with the hairs of her head. Thou gavest me no kiss: but this woman since the time I came in hath not ceased to kiss my feet. And with oil thou didst not anoint me. But this woman hath anointe My head with oil, and poured ointment on my feet. Wherefore I say unto thee,**

Her sins, which are many, are forgiven; for she loved much: but to whom little is forgiven, the same loveth little. And he said unto her, Thy sins are forgiven. And they that sat at meat with him began to say within themselves, Who is this that forgiveth sins also? And he said to the woman, **Thy faith hath saved thee; go in peace.**

WOMEN ACCOMPANY JESUS
AND THE DISCIPLES

And it came to pass afterward, that he went throughout every city and village, preaching and showing the glad tidings of the kingdom of God: and the twelve were with him, and certain women, which had been healed of evil spirits and infirmities, Mary called Magdalene, out of whom went seven devils, and Joanna the wife of Chuza Herod's steward, and Susanna, and many others, which ministered unto him of their substance.

Religious Leaders Accuse Jesus of Being Satan

And the multitude cometh together again, so that they could not so much as eat bread.

Then was brought unto him one possessed with a devil, blind and dumb, and he healed him, insomuch that the blind and dumb both spake and saw. And all the people were amazed, and said, Is not this the son of David? But when the Pharisees and scribes which came down from Jerusalem heard of it, they said, This fellow doth not he casteth out devils, by Beelzebub, the prince of the devils. And when his friends heard of it, they went out to lay hold on him: for they said, He is beside himself. And Jesus knowing their thoughts, called them unto him, and spoke to them in parables.

How can Satan cast out Satan? Every kingdom divided against itself is brought to desolation; and cannot stand. And every city or house divided against itself shall not stand: And if Satan cast out Satan, he is divided against himself; how shall then his kingdom stand? And if I by Beelzebub cast out devils, by whom do your children cast them out? Therefore they shall be your judges.

But if I cast out devils by the Spirit of God, then the kingdom of God is come unto you. Or else how can one enter into a strong man's house, and spoil his goods, except he first bind the strong man? and then he will spoil his house. He that is not with me is against me: and he that gathereth not with me scattereth abroad. Wherefore I say unto you, All manner of sin and blasphemy shall be forgiven unto men: But the blasphemy against the Holy Ghost

shall not be forgiven unto men. And whosoever speaketh a word against the Son of man, it shall be forgiven him: but whosoever speaketh against the Holy Ghost, it shall not be forgiven him, neither in this world, neither in the world to come. Either make the tree good, and his fruit good; or else make the tree corrupt, and his fruit corrupt: for the tree is known by his fruit. O generation of vipers, how can ye, being evil, speak good things?

For out of the abundance of the heart the mouth speaketh. A good man out of the good treasure of the heart bringeth forth good things: and an evil man out of the evil treasure bringeth forth evil things. But I say unto you, That every idle word that men shall speak, they shall give account thereof in the day of judgment. For by thy words thou shalt be justified, and by thy words thou shalt be condemned.

Religious Leaders ask Jesus for a Miracle

Then certain of the scribes and of the Pharisees answered, saying, Master, we would that thou would give us a sign. But he answered and said unto them, **An evil and adulterous generation seeketh after a sign; and there shall no sign be given unto it, but the sign of the prophet Jonas: For as Jonas was three days and three nights in the whale's belly; so shall the Son of man be three days and three nights in the heart of the earth. The men of Nineveh shall rise in judgment with this generation, and shall condemn it: because they repented at the preaching of Jonas; and, behold, one greater than Jonas is here. The queen of the south shall rise up in the judgment with this generation, and shall condemn it: for she came from the uttermost parts of the earth to hear the wisdom of Solomon; and, behold, a greater than Solomon is here. When the unclean spirit is gone out of a man, he walketh through dry places, seeking rest, and findeth none. Then he saith, I will return into my house from whence I came out; and when he is come, he findeth it empty, swept, and garnished. Then goethhe,andtakethwithhimselfsevenotherspiritsmore wicked than himself, and they enter in and dwell there: and the last state of that man is worse than the first. Even so shall it be also unto this wicked generation.**

Jesus Describes His True Family

While he yet talked unto the people, came then his brethren and his mother, and could not come to him for the press. And it was told him by certain of them which saith, Thy mother and thy brethren standth without, desiring to see thee. And as the multitude sat he looked round about them, and stretched forth his hand toward his disciples, and spoke unto them. **Who is my mother? And who are my brethren? For behold whosoever shall hear the word and doth it, does the will of my Father which is in heaven, the same is my brother, and sister, and mother.**

Jesus Tells the Parable
of the Four Soil's

On that same day when much people were gathered together, and came to him out of every city, Jesus went out of the house, and began to teach them, but because of the great multude, He got into a ship, and pushed out from shore. And all the people stood at the shore. And He spake in his doctrine, many things unto them in parables, saying, **Behold, there went out a sower to sow his seed, and it came to pass, as he sowed, some fell by the way side, and were trodden down and the fowls of the air came and devoured them up. And some fell on stony ground, where it had not much earth: and immediately it sprang up, and it withered away when the sun came up. Because it had no root and lacked moisture. And other fell among thorns, and as they grew up, were choked by them, and could not yielded its fruit. But others fell into good ground and brought forth much fruit, yielding up and increasing. Some thirty, and some sixty, and some hundredfold.** And he said unto them, **He that hath ears to hear, let him hear.**

Jesus Explains Parable
of the Sower

And when he was alone, they that were with him and the twelve asked of him; Why speakiest thou in parables? **Unto you it is given to know the mystery of the kingdom of God: but unto them that are without, all these things are done in parables: That seeing they may see, and not perceive; and hearing they may hear, and not understand; lest at any time they should be converted, and their sins should be forgiven them. No man, when he hath lighted a candle, covereth it with a vessel. Or putteth it under a bed; but setteth it on a candlestick, that they which enter in may see the light. For nothing is done in secret, that shall not be made known; neither any thing hid, that shall not be uncovered and reviled to all.**

For whosoever hath, to him shall be given, and he shall have more abundance: but whosoever hath not, from him shall be taken away even that he hath.

To them is fulfilled the prophecy of Esaias. *For this people's heart is waxed cold, and their ears are dull of hearing. Because Satan cometh immediately, and taketh away the word that was sown in their hearts that I should heal them. But blessed are your eyes, for they see: and your ears, for they hear.* For verily I say unto you, That many prophets and righteous have desired to see those things which ye see, and have not seen them, and to hear those things which ye hear, and have not heard them.

Hear ye therefore the parable of the sower. When any one heareth the word of the kingdom, and understandeth it not, then cometh the wicked one, and catcheth away that which was sown in his heart. This is he which received seed by the way side. But he that received the seed into stony places, the same is he that heareth the word, and with joy receiveth it: Yet hath he not root in himself, but dureth for a while: for when tribulation or persecution ariseth because of the word, by and by he is offended. He also that received seed among the thorns is he that heareth the word; and the cares of this world, and the deceitfulness of riches, choke the word, and he becometh unfruitful. But he that received seed into the good ground is he that heareth the word, and understandeth it; Is He which also beareth fruit, and bringeth forth, some an hundredfold, some sixty, some thirty.

Parable of the Growing Seed

The kingdom of God is as if a man should scatter seed apond the ground, and sleepth by night, and rise by day, and the seed spouth and grow, he himself knowth not how. For the earth yields crops by itself: first the blade, then head, after that the full grain in the head. But when the grain ripens, immediately he puts it to the sickle, because the harvest has come.

Parable of the Weeds

Another parable put he forth unto them, saying, **The kingdom of heaven is likened unto a man which sowed good seed in his field: But while he slept, his enemy came and sowed tares among the wheat, and went his way. But when the blade was sprung up, and brought forth fruit, then appeared the tares also. So the servants of the householder came and said unto him, Sir, didst not thou sow good seed in thy field? from whence then hath it tares? He said unto them, an enemy hath done this. The servants said unto him, Wilt thou then that we go and gather them up? But he said, Nay; lest while ye gather up the tares. Ye root up also the wheat with them. So let both grow together until the harvest: and in the time of harvest I will say unto the reapers, gather ye together first the tares, and bind them in bundles to burn them: but gather the wheat into my barn.**

Parable of Mustard Seed

Another parable put he forth unto them, saying, **Were unto shall we liken the kingdom of God? Or with what comparison shall we compare it?**

It is like a grain of mustard seed, which, when it is sown in the earth, is the lest of all the seeds that be in the earth: But when it is sown, it growth up, and becometh greater than all herbs, and shooteth out great branches; so that the fowls of the air may lodge under the shadow of it. And with many such parables spake he the word unto them, as they were able to hear it. But without a parable spake he not unto them: and when they were alone, he expounded all things unto his disciples.

Jesus tells Parable of the yeast

Another parable spake he unto them; **The kingdom of heaven is like unto leaven, which a woman took, and hid in three measures of meal, till the whole was leavened.** All these things spake Jesus unto the multitude in parables; and without a parable spake he not unto them: That it might be fulfilled which was spoken by the prophet, saying, *I will open my mouth in parables; I will utter things which have been kept secret from the foundation of the world.* Then Jesus sent the multitude away, and went into the house: and his disciples came unto him, saying, declare unto us the parable of the tares of the field.

Jesus Explains The Parable of tares

He answered and said unto them, **He that soweth the good seed is the Son of man; The field is the world; the good seed are the children of the kingdom; but the tares are the children of the wicked one; The enemy that sowed them is the devil; the harvest is the end of the world; and the reapers are the angels. As therefore the tares are gathered and burned in the fire; so shall it be in the end of this world.**

The Son of man shall send forth his angels, and they shall gather out of his kingdom all things that offend, and them which do iniquity; And shall cast them into a furnace of fire: there shall be wailing and gnashing of teeth.

Then shall the righteous shine forth as the sun in the kingdom of their Father. Who hath ears to hear, let him hear. Again, the kingdom of heaven is like unto treasure hid in a field; the which when a man hath found, he hideth, and for joy thereof goeth and selleth all that he hath, and buyeth that field.

Jesus Tells of Hidden Treasure

The Pearl Merchant Parable of the Fishing Net

Again, the kingdom of heaven is like unto a merchant man, seeking goodly pearls: Who, when he had found one pearl of great price, went and sold all that he had, and bought it. Again, the kingdom of heaven is like unto a net, that was cast into the sea, and gathered of every kind fish. Which, when it was full, they drew to shore, and sat down, and gathered the good into the vessels, but cast the bad away. So shall it be at the end of the world: the angels shall come forth, and sever the wicked from among the just, And shall cast them into the furnace of fire; there shall be wailing and gnashing of teeth. Jesus saith unto them, **Have ye understood all these things?** They say unto him, Yea, Lord. Then said he unto them, **Therefore every scribe which is instructed unto the kingdom of heaven is like unto a man that is an householder, which bringeth forth out of his treasure things new and old.**

Jesus Calms the Storm

Now it came to pass on a certain day, after they sent the multitudes away, when evening was come that he went into a ship with his disciples: and he said unto them, **Let us go over unto the other side of the lake.** And they launched forth, but as they sailed he fell asleep: And behold, there arose a great tempest in the sea, insomuch that the ship was shaken by the wind and covered with the waves that beat upon it. So that it was filling up with water. And they were in jeopardy.

And Jesus being in the hinder part of the ship sleeping on a pillow: And his disciples came to him, and awoke him, saying, Lord, save us: Carest thou not that we perish. Then he arose, rebuked the wind and said unto the sea, **Peace, be still.** And the wind ceased, and the water grew still and there was a great calm. Then he said unto them**, why are you so fearful, O ye of little faith. How is it that ye have no faith?** But fearing exceedingly, they said one to another, what manner of man is this, that even the wind and the sea obey him? And they marveled.

Jesus Sends the Demons into a Herd of Pigs

And when he was come to the other side of the sea, into the country of the Gergesenes, which is over against Galilee. He went forth out of the ship, immediately there met him out of the city two possessed with devils, unclean spirits, Which had been tormented a long time, and wore no clothes, neither abode in any house, but had their dwelling among the tombs:

No man could bind them, not even with chains: Because they had been often bound with fetters and chains, and the chains were plucked asunder by them, and the fetters broken in pieces: neither could any man tame them. And always, night and day, they were in the mountains, and in the tombs, crying, and cutting themselves with stones.

But when they saw Jesus afar off, they ran and worshiped him, And cried with a loud voice, saying What have we to do with thee, **Jesus,** thou *Son of the most high God?* We beseech thee, torment us not, For Jesus had said unto them, **Come out of them, thou unclean spirit**, and he asked them, **What is thy name?**

And they answered, saying, my name is legion: for we are many. And they asked of him, much that he would not send them away out of the country. Now there was there nigh unto the mountains a great herd of swine feeding. And all the devils besought him, saying, Send us into the swine, that we may enter into them. And forthwith Jesus gave them leave; and the unclean spirits went out, and entered into the swine: and the herd ran violently down a steep place into the sea, about two thousand: and perished in the waters.

And they that fed the swine fled, and told it in the city, and in the country. And they came unto Jesus, and seeing them that was possessed with the devils, the legion of unclean spirits sitting, and clothed, and in their right mind: and they were afraid, and they that saw it told them how it befell to them that was possessed with the devils and also concerning the swine.

And they began to ask him to depart out of their coasts. And when he was come into the ship, those that had been possessed with the devils prayed him that they might be with him. Howbeit Jesus suffered them not, but saith unto them, **Go home to thy friends, and tell them how great things the Lord hath done for thee, and hath had compassion on thee.** And they departed, and began to publish in Decapolis how great things Jesus had done for them, and all men did marvel.

Jesus Heals a Bleeding Woman

Restores a Girl to Life

And when Jesus was passed over again by ship unto the other side, the people gladly received him: for they were waiting for him. And much people gathered unto him: and he was nigh unto the sea. And, behold, there cometh one of the rulers of the synagogue, Jairus by name; and when he saw him, he fell at his feet, And besought him greatly, saying, my little daughter lieth at the point of death: I pray thee, come unto my house and lay thy hands on her, that she may be healed; and shall live. For he had only one daughter, about twelve years of age, and she lay a dying. And Jesus went with him; and much people followed him, and thronged him.

And behold a certain woman, which had an issue of blood, twelve years, and had suffered many things by many physicians, spent all that she had, and was nothing bettered, but rather grew worse, When she had heard of Jesus, she came in the press behind him, and touched his garment, For she said, if I only touch but his clothes, I shall be whole. And immediately her issue of blood was dried up; and she felt in her body that she was healed of that plague. Jesus, immediately knowing in himself that virtue had gone out of him, turned him about in the press, and said, **Who touched my clothes?**

When all denied, Peter and the other disciples said unto him, Master, Thou seeth the multitude thronging thee, and sayest thou, Who touched me? And he looked round about to see who had done this thing. Somebody hath touched me: And when the woman saw that she was not hid, fearing and trembling knowing what was done in her, came and fell down before him, declaring unto him, before all the people for what cause she had touched him, and how she was healed immediately. And he said unto her, **Daughter, be of good comfort: thy faith hath made thee whole; go in peace.**

While he yet spake, there cometh one from the ruler of the synagogues house, saying to Jairus, Thy daughter is dead; trouble not the Master, But when Jesus heard it, he answered him, saying, **Fear not: believe only, and she shall be made whole.** And when he was

come unto the house, he saith unto them, **Why make ye this ado, and weep? The damsel is not dead, but sleepeth.** And they laughed him to scorn, knowing that she was dead. But when the people were put forth, he went in, with the damsel's father and mother and enterth in where the damsel was lying, took her by the hand, and said unto her, **Talitha cumi;** which is, being interpreted, Damsel, **I say unto thee, arise.** And straightway the damsel arose, and walked; and they were astonished with a great astonishment. Then he charged them straitly that no man should know it; and commanded that something should be given her to eat. But the fame thereof went abroad into all that land.

Jesus Heals the Blind and Mute

And when Jesus departed thence, two blind men followed him, crying, and saying, Thou Son of David, have mercy on us. And when he was come into the house, the blind men came to him: and Jesus saith unto him, **Believe ye that I am able to do this?** They said unto him, Yea, Lord. Then touched he their eyes, saying, **According to your faith be it unto you.** And their eyes were opened; and Jesus straitly charged them, saying, **See that no man know it.** But when they were departed, spread abroad his fame in all that country. As they went out, behold, they brought to him a dumb man possessed with a devil. And when the devil was cast out, the dumb spake: and the multitudes marveled, saying, It was never so seen in Israel. But the Pharisees said, He casteth out devils through the prince of the devils.

People of Nazareth Refuse to Believe

And it came to pass, that when Jesus had finished these parables, he departed thence. Coming into his own country, and when the sabbath day was come, he began to teach in the synagogue: and all that heard him were astonished, saying, From whence hath this man these things? And what wisdom is this which is given unto him, that even such mighty works are wrought by his hands? Is not this the carpenter's son? Is not his mother called *Mary*? And his brethren, James, and Joses, and Simon, and Judas? And his sisters, are they not all with us? And they were offended in him. But Jesus said unto them, **A prophet is not without honor, save and among his own house, kin, and in his own country,** And he could there do no mighty work, save that he laid his hands upon a few sick folk, and healed them. And he marvelled because of their unbelief. So he left and went round to other villages, teaching.

Urges the Disciples to Pray for the Workers

And Jesus went about all the cities and villages, teaching in their synagogues, and preaching the gospel of the kingdom, and healing every sickness and every disease among the people. But when he saw the multitudes, he was moved with compassion on them, because they fainted, and were scattered abroad, as sheep having no shepherd. Then saith he unto his disciples, **The harvest truly is plenteous, but the laborers are few; Pray ye therefore the Lord of the harvest, that he will send forth laborers into his harvest.**

Jesus Sends Out the Twelve

And when he had called unto him his twelve disciples, he gave them power, and authority over all unclean spirits, to cast them out, and to heal all manner of sickness and disease.

Now the names of the twelve apostles are these; the first, Simon, who is called *Peter*, and *Andrew* his brother; *James* the son of Zebedee, and *John* his brother; *Philip,* and *Bartholomew*; *Thomas,* and *Matthew* the publican; *James* the son of Alphaeus, and Lebbaeus, whose surname was *Thaddaeus;* Simon the Canaanite, and *Judas Iscariot,* who also betrayed him.

These twelve Jesus sent forth, and commanded them, saying, **Go not into the way of the Gentiles, and into any city of the Samaritans enter ye not: But go rather to the lost sheep of the house of Israel. And as ye go, preach, saying, The kingdom of heaven is at hand. Heal the sick, cleanse the lepers, raise the dead, cast out devils: freely ye have received, freely give. Provide neither gold, nor silver, or brass in your purses. Nor scrip for your journey, neither two coats, neither shoes, nor yet staves: for the workman is worthy of his meat. And into whatsoever city or town ye shall enter, enquire who in it is worthy; and there abide till ye go thence. And when ye come into and house, salute it. And if the house be worthy, let your peace come upon it: but if it be not worthy, let your peace return unto you. And whosoever shall not receive you, nor hear your words, when ye depart out of that house or city, shake off the dust of your feet, for a testimony against them. Verily I say unto you, it shall be more tolerable for the land of Sodom and**

Gomorrha in the day of Judgment, than for that city. And they departed, and went through the towns, preaching the gospel, that men should repent. And they cast out many devils, and anointed with oil many that were sick, and healed them.

Jesus Prepares Disciples
for Persecution

Behold, I send you forth as sheep in the midst of wolves: be ye therefore wise as serpents, and harmless as doves. But beware of men: for they will deliver you up to the councils, and they will scourge you in their synagogues; And ye shall be brought before governors and kings for my sake, for a testimony against them and the Gentiles. But when they deliver you up, take no thought how or what ye shall speak: for it shall be given you in that same hour what ye shall speak. For it is not ye that speak, but the Spirit of your Father which speaketh in you. And the brother shall deliver up the brother unto death, and the father the child: and the children shall rise up against their parents, and cause them to be put to death. And ye shall be hated of all men for my name's sake: but he that endureth to the end shall be saved. But when they persecute you in this city, flee ye into another: for verily I say unto you, Ye shall not have gone over the cities of Israel, till the Son of man shell come. The disciple is not above his master, nor the servant above his lord. It is enough for the disciple that he be as his master, and the servant as his lord. If they have called the master of the house Beelzebub, how much more shall they call them of his household? Fear them not therefore: for there is nothing covered, that shall not be revealed; and hid, that shall not be known.

What I tell you in darkness, that speak ye in light: and what ye hear in the ear, that preach ye upon the housetops. And fear not them which kill the body, but are not able to kill the soul: but rather fear him which is able to destroy both soul and body in hell. Are not two sparrows sold for a farthing? and one of them shall not fall on the ground without your Father.

But the very hairs of your head are all numbered. Fear ye not therefore, ye are of more value than many sparrows. Whosoever therefore shall confess me before men, him will I confess also before my Father which is in heaven. But whosoever shall deny me before men, him will I also deny before my Father which is in heaven. Think not that I am come to send peace on earth: I came not to send peace, but a sword. For I am come to set a man at variance against his father, and the daughter against her mother, and the daughter in law against her mother in law. And a man's foes shall be they of his own household. He that loveth father or mother more than me is not worthy of me: and he that loveth son or daughter more than me is not worthy of me. And he that taketh not his cross, and followeth after me, is not worthy of me. He that findeth his life shall lose it: and he that loseth his life for my sake shall find it. He that receiveth you receiveth me, and he that receiveth me receiveth him that sent me. He that receiveth a prophet in the name of a prophet shall receive a prophet's reward; and he that receiveth a righteous man in the name of a righteous man shall receive a righteous man's reward. And whosoever shall give to drink unto one of these little ones a cup of cold water because he is my disciple, verily I say unto you, he shall in no wise lose his reward.

Herod Kills John the Baptist

Now Herod the tetrarch heard of the fame of Jesus (for his name was spread abroad:) and he was perplexed, because that it was said of some, that John was risen from the dead; and others that Elijah had appeared, and still others that one of the prophets of long ago had come back from the dead, therefore mighty works do show forth themselves in him. For Herod had laid hold on John, and bound him, and put him in prison for Herodias' sake, his Brother Philip's wife: for he had married her. For John had said unto Herod, It is not lawful for thee to have thy brother's wife. Therefore Herodias had a quarrel against him, and would have killed him; but she could not: For Herod feared John, knowing that he was a just and holy man, and observed him; and when he heard how he did many things, He went to him gladly.

And when a convenient day was come, on Herod's birthday, he made a supper unto his lords, high captains, and chief estates of Galilee; And when the daughter of the said Herodias came in, and danced, and pleased Herod and them that sat with him, the king said unto the damsel, Ask of me whatsoever thou wilt, and I will give it unto thee. And he swore unto her, whatsoever thou shalt ask of me, I will give it thee, unto the half of my kingdom. And she went forth, and said unto her mother, What shall I ask? And she said, the head of John the Baptist. And she came in straightway with haste unto the king, and asked, saying, I will that thou give me here John Baptist's head in a charger. And the king was exceeding sorry; yet for his oath's sake, and for their sakes which sat with him, he would not reject her.

And immediately the king sent an executioner, and commanded his head to be brought: and he went and beheaded him in the prison, and brought his head in a charger, and gave it unto the damsel: and the damsel gave it unto her mother. And when his disciples heard of it, they came and took up his corpse, and laid it in a tomb.

Jesus Feeds Five Thousand

When they returned, the apostles gathered themselves together unto Jesus, and told him all things, both what they had done, and what they had taught. And Then came word of John's death, He said unto them, **Come ye yourselves apart into a desert place, and rest a while,** for there were many coming and going, for they had no leisure so much as to eat. So they departed thence by ship over the sea of Galilee, which is the sea of Tiberias; to desert place, privately belonging to the city called Bethsaida,. Jesus went up into a mountain, and there he sat with his disciples. And when the people, a great multitude, heard thereof, they followed him on foot out of the cities. And when Jesus went forth, and saw the great multitude, he was moved with compassion toward them, and received them, healing their sick because they were as sheep not having a shepherd: and he began to teach them many things.

The Passover, a feast of the Jews, was nigh. Jesus then lifted up his eyes, and saw the great company, He saith unto Philip, **Whence shall we by bread, that these may eat? For the time is past; and evening, is come,** he said this to prove him: for he himself knew what he would do.

Philip and disciples said send the multitude away that they may go into the villages, countryside round about, and by themselves victuals. Jesus said unto them, **They need not depart; give ye them to eat.**

Andrew, Simon Peter's brother, saith unto him, we have here but five loaves, and two fishes. Two hundred pennyworth of bread is not sufficient for them, that every one of them may take a little. And Jesus said, **Make the men sit down.**

Now there was much grass in the place. He commanded them to sit down by companies upon the grass. So the men sat down, in ranks, by hundreds, and by fifties. And when he had taken the five loaves and two fishes, he looked up to heaven, and blessed them, broke the loaves, and gave them to his disciples to set before them: and the two fishes: when they were filled, he said unto his disciples, **Gather fragments that remain, that nothing be lost.**

Therefore they gathered them together, and filled twelve baskets with the fragments of the five barley loaves, which remained over and above unto them that had eaten. And they that had eaten were about five thousand men, beside women and children. And those men, that had seen the miracle that Jesus did said, this is of a truth that prophet that should come into the world.

When Jesus therefore perceived that they would come and take him by force, to make him a king, he departed again into a mountain himself alone.

Jesus Walks on Water

Jesus constrained his disciples to get into a ship, and to go before him unto the other side, unto Bethsaida, while he sent the multitudes away. He went up into a mountain apart to pray: and when the evening was come, he was there alone.

And he saw them toiling and rowing; for the wind was contrary unto them, being tossed with the waves: when they had rowed about five and twenty or thirty furlongs, Jesus in the fourth watch of the night, came unto them, walking on the sea, and would have passed by them. But when they saw him walking upon the sea, they were greatly troubled, saying, It is a spirit; and they cried out for fear. As Jesus drawing nigh unto the ship: he spake unto them, saying, **Be of good cheer; it is I; be not afraid**. And Peter answered him and said, Lord, if it be thou, bid me come unto thee on the water. And he said, **Come.** And when Peter was come down out of the ship, he walked on the water, to go to Jesus. But when he saw the how boisterous the wind, he was afraid; and beginning to sink, he cried out saying, Lord, save me. And immediately Jesus stretched forth his hand, caught him, and said unto him, **O thou of little faith, wherefore didst thou doubt?** And when they were come into the ship, they willingly received him and worshipped him, saying, Of a truth thou art the Son of God. They were sore amazed in themselves beyond measure, and wondered. For they considered not the miracle of the loaves: for their heart was hardened.

Jesus Heals All Who Touch Him

And when they had passed over, they came into the land of Gennesaret, and drew near to the shore. And when they were come out of the ship, straightway they knew him, and ran through that whole region round about, and began to carry in beds of those that were sick and diseased; where they heard he was. And whithersoever he entered, into villages, or cities, or country, they laid the sick in the streets, and besought him that they might touch if it were but the border of his garment: and as many as touched him were made perfectly whole.

Jesus Is the True Bread
from Heaven

The day following, when the people which stood on the other side of the sea saw that there was no other boat there, save that one where into his disciples were entered, and that Jesus went not with his disciples into the boat, but that his disciples were gone away alone; (Howbeit there came other boats from Tiberias nigh unto the place where they did eat bread, after that the Lord had given thanks:)

When the people therefore saw that Jesus was not there, neither his disciples, they also took boats, and came to Capernaum, seeking for Jesus. And when they had found him on the other side of the sea, they said unto him, Rabbi, when camest thou hither? Jesus answered them and said, **Verily, verily, I say unto you, Ye seek me, not because ye saw the miracles, but because ye did eat of the loaves, and were filled. Labour not for the meat which perisheth, but for that meat which endureth unto everlasting life, which the Son of man shall give unto you: for him hath God the Father sealed.**

Then said they unto him, what shall we do, that we might work the works of God? Jesus answered and said unto them, **This is the work of God, that ye believe on him whom he hath sent.** They said therefore unto him, what sign showest thou then, that we may see, and believe thee? what work will thou do?

Our fathers did eat manna in the desert; as it is written, He gave them bread from heaven to eat. Then Jesus said unto them, **Verily, verily, I say unto you, Moses gave ye not that bread from heaven; but my Father giveth you the true bread from heaven. For the** bread of God is he which cometh down from heaven, and giveth life unto the world.

Then said they unto him, Lord, evermore give us this bread. And Jesus said unto them, **I am the bread of life: he that cometh to me shall never hunger; and he that believeth on me shall never thirst. But I said unto you, That ye also have seen me, and believe not. All that the Father giveth me shall come unto me; and him that cometh to me I will in no wise cast out. For I came down from heaven, not to do mine own will, but the will of him that sent me.**

And this is the Father's will which hath sent me, that of all which he hath given me I should lose nothing, but should raise it up again at the last day. And this is the will of him that sent me, that every one which seeth the Son, and believeth upond him, may have everlasting life: and I will raise him up at the last day. The Jews then murmured at him, because he said, I am the bread which came down from heaven. And they said, Is not this Jesus, the son of Joseph, whose father and mother we knowth? how is it then that he saith, I came down from heaven?

Jews Disagree That Jesus Is from Heaven

Jesus therefore answered and said unto them, **Murmur not among yourselves. No man can come unto me, except the Father which hath sent me drawth him: and I will raise him up at the last day. It is written in the prophets, and they shall be all taught of God. Every man therefore that hath heard, and hath learned of the Father, cometh unto me. Not that any man hath seen the Father, save he which is of God, he hath seen the Father. Verily, verily, I say unto you, He that believeth on me hath everlasting life. I am that bread of life. Your fathers did eat manna in the wilderness, and are dead. This is the bread which cometh down from heaven, that a man may eat thereof, and not die. I am the living bread which came down from heaven: if any man eat of this bread, he shall live for ever: and the bread that I will giveth is my flesh, which I will give for the life of the world.**

The Jews therefore strove among themselves, saying, How can this man give us his flesh to eat? Then Jesus said unto them, **Verily, verily, I say unto you, Except ye eat the flesh of the Son of man, and drink his blood, ye have no life in with you. Whoso eateth my flesh, and drinketh my blood, hath eternal life; and I will raise him up at the last day. For my flesh is meat, and my blood is drink indeed. He that eateth my flesh, and drinketh my blood, dwelleth in me, and I in him. As the living Father hath sent me, and I live by the Father: so he that eateth me, even he shall live by me. This is that bread which came down from heaven: not as your fathers did eat manna, and are dead: he that eateth of this bread shall live for ever.** These things said he in the synagogue, as he taught in Capernaum.

MANY DISCIPLES DESERT JESUS

Therefore many of His disciples, when they heard this, said, "This is a hard saying; who can understand it?" When Jesus knew in Himself that His disciples complained about this, He said unto them, **"Does this offend you? What then if you should see the Son of Man ascend where He was before? It is the Spirit who gives life; the flesh profits nothing. The words that I speak unto you are of the spirit, and they are life. But there are some of you who doth not believe."** For Jesus knew from the beginning who they were who did not believe, and who would betrayth Him. And He said, **"Therefore I have said to you that no one can come unto Me unless it has been granted unto him by My Father."** From that time many of His disciples went back and walked no more with Him. Then Jesus said unto the twelve, **"Do you also want to goth away?"** But Simon Peter answered Him, *"Lord,* to whom shall we goth? For you have the words of eternal life. Also we have come to believe and know that You are the Christ, the Son of the living God." Jesus, answered them, **"Did I not choose you, the twelve, and one of you is a devil?"** He spake of Judas Iscariot, the son of Simon, for it was he who would betrayed Him, being one of the twelve.

Jesus Teaches about Inner Purity

Then came together unto him the Pharisees, and certain of the scribes, which came from Jerusalem. And when they saw some of his disciples eat bread with defiled hands, that is to say, with unwashed hands, they found fault. For the Pharisees, and all the Jews, except they wash their hand often, when they come from the market places, eat not, holding the tradition of the elders. And many other things there be, which they have received to hold, as the washing of cups, and pots, brasen vessels, and of tables. Then the Pharisees and scribes asked him, why walk not thy disciples according to the tradition of the elders, but eat bread with unwashed hands? He answered and said unto them, **Well hath Esaias prophesied of you hypocrite, as it is written, This people honoureth me with their lips, but their heart is far from me. Howbeit in vain do they worship me, teaching of the doctrines and commandments of men. For laying aside the commandment of God, ye hold the tradition of men, as the washing of pots and cups: and many other such like things ye do. And he said unto them, Full well ye reject the commandment of God, that ye may keep your own tradition. For Moses said, Honor thy father and thy mother; and Whoso curseth father or mother, let him be put to death: But ye say, if a man shall say unto his father or mother, It is Corban, that is to say, a gift, by whatsoever thou mightiest be profited by me; he shall be free. And ye suffer him no more to do ought for his father or his mother; Making the word of God of none effect through your tradition, which ye have delivered: and many such like things do ye.**

And he called the multitude, and said unto them, **Hear, and understand: Not that which goeth into the mouth defileth a man; but that which cometh out of the mouth, this defileth a man.** Then came his disciples, and said unto him, Knowest thou that the Pharisees were offended, after they heard this saying? But he answered and said, **Every plant, which my heavenly Father hath not planted, shall be rooted up. Let them alone: they be blind leaders of the blind. And if the blind lead the blind, both shall fall into the ditch.**

And then they entered into the house away from the people, Peter, and the disciples asked him concerning the parable. And he said unto them, **Are ye so without understanding also? Do ye not perceive, that whatsoever thing from without entereth into the man, it cannot defile him; Because it enterth not into his heart, but into the belly, and goeth out into the draught, purging all meats?** And he said, **That which cometh out of the man's heart that defileth a man. For from within, out of the heart of men, proceed evil thoughts, fornications, murders, thefts, covetousness, wickedness, deceit, lasciviousness, and evil eye, blasphemy, pride, foolishness: All these evil things come from within, and defile the man.**

Jesus Sends Demon Out of a Girl

And from thence he arose, and went into the borders of Tyre and Sidon, and entered into an house, and would have no man know it: but he could not be hid.

Then a certain woman of Canaan, she a Greek, Syrophenician by nation; came and fell at Jesus feet, crying unto him, saying, Have mercy on me, O Lord, thou Son of David; my daughter is grievously vexed with a devil. But he answered not a word. And his disciples came and besought him, saying, Send her away; for she crieth after us. Then Jesus said unto her **Let the children first be filled: I am not sent but unto the lost sheep of the house of Israel.** Then she worshipped him, saying, Lord, help me. I know ye speak truth, yet the dogs under the table eat of the crumbs which fall from their masters' table, Jesus answered her and said unto her, **O woman, great is thy faith: be it unto thee even as thou wilt. The devil is gone out of thy daughter.** And when she was come unto her house, she found her daughter lying upon the bed, the devil gone out from her daughter was made whole that very hour.

The crowd marvels At Jesus,
healing

And again departing from the coasts of Tyre and Sidon, he came unto the sea of Galilee, through the midst of the coasts of Decapolis. And great multitudes came unto him, bringing those that were, lame, blind, maimed, and may others, and cast them down at Jesus' feet; and he healed them: They baring unto him one that was deaf, and had an impediment in his speech; and they beseech him to put his hand upon him. And he took him aside from the multitude, and put his fingers into his ears, and he spit, and touched his tongue; And looking up to heaven, he sighed, and saith unto him, **Ephphatha,** that is be opened. And straightway his ears were opened, and the string of his tongue was loosed, and he spake plain. And he charged them that they should tell no man: but the more he charged them, so much the more a great deal they published it. And they were beyond measure astonished, saying, He hath done all things well: he maketh both the deaf to hear, and the dumb to speak.

Jesus Feeds the Four Thousand

In those days the multitude being very great and having nothing to eat, Jesus called his disciples unto him, and saith unto them, **I have compassion on the multitude, because they have now been with me three days, and have nothing to eat: And if I send them away fasting to their own houses, they may faint in the way.** And his disciples answered him, from whence can a man satisfy these men with bread here in wilderness? And he asked them, **How many loaves have ye?**

And they said, seven, and a few little fishes. So he commanded the people to sit down on the ground: and he took the seven loaves and the fishes, and gave thanks, and broke them, and gave unto his disciples, to set before them; and they did all eat, and were filled: and they took up of the broken meat that was left seven baskets full. And they that did eat were four thousand men, beside women and children. And then he had sent away the multitude, and straightway he entered into a ship with his disciples, and came to the coast of Maglala, into the parts of Dalmanutha.

Religious Leaders Ask for a Sign

And the Pharisees also with the Sadducees came, tempting, desired him that he would show them a sign from heaven. He sighed deeply in his spirit, and saith unto them, **Why doth this generation seek after a sign? Verily I say unto you, There shall no sign be given unto this generation, but the sign of the prophet Jonas.**

For as Jones was three days and three nights in the whales belly; so shall the Son be three days and three nights in the heart of the earth. The men of Nineveh shall rise up judgment with generation, and shall condemn it: because they repented at the preaching of Jonas; and behold a greater then he is here.

When it is evening, ye say, it will be fair weather: for the sky is red. And in the morning, it will be foul weather to day: for the sky is red and lowing. O ye hypocrites, ye can discern the face of the sky; but can ye not discern the signs of the times? A wicked and adulterous generation seeketh after a sign.

Jesus Warns of Wrong Teaching

And when his disciples were come to the other side, they had forgotten to take bread. Neither had they in the ship with them more than one loaf. Then Jesus said unto them, **Take heed and beware of the leaven of the Pharisees and of the Sadducees, as well of the leaven of Herod**.

And they reasoned among themselves, saying, It is because we have taken no bread. Which when Jesus perceived, their thoughts, he said unto them, **Why reason ye among yourselves, because ye have no bread? O ye of little faith, Perceive ye not yet, neither understand? Have ye your hearts so yet been hardened? Having eyes see ye not? And having ears, hear ye not? And do yet not remember? When I broke the five loaves among five thousand, How many baskets full of fragments took ye up?** They said unto him, Twelve. **And when the seven among four thousand, how many baskets full of fragments took ye up?** And they said Seven. **How is it that ye do not understand that I spake it not to you concerning bread, but that ye should beware of the leaven of the Pharisees and of the Sadducees?** Then understood they how that he bade them not beware of the leaven of bread, but of the doctrine of the Pharisees and of the Sadducees.

Jesus Restores Sight to a Blind Man

And he cometh to Bethsaida; and they broth unto him a blind man, and besought him to touch him. And he took the blind man by the hand, and led him out of town; and when he had spit on his eyes, and put his hands upon him, he asked him **if he saw ought.** And he looked up, and said, I see men as trees, walking. After that he put his hands again upon his eyes, and made him look up: and saw every man clearly. And he sent him away to his house, saying, **neither go into the town, nor tell it to any in the town.**

Jesus Asks His Disciples Whom do men say that I am

And it came to pass, as he was alone praying, He got up, called his disciples and went out, into the towns of Caesarea Philppi: and by the way he asked his disciples, saying unto them, **Whom do men say that I the Son of man am?** And they answered, Some say that thou art John the Baptist come back to life, but some say Elias; and others Jeremias, or one of the prophets, is risen again. And he saith unto them, **But whom say ye that I am?** And Peter answereth and saith unto him, Thou art the Christ, the Son of the living God.

Jesus answered and said unto him, **Blessed art thou, Simon Barjona: for flesh and blood hath not revealed it unto thee, but my Father which is in heaven. And I say also unto thee, That thou art Peter, and upon this rock I will build my church; and the gates of hell shall not prevail against it. And I will give unto thee the keys of the kingdom of heaven: and whatsoever thou shalt bind on earth shall be bound in heaven: and whatsoever thou shalt loose on earth shall be loosed in heaven.** Then charged he his disciples that they should tell no man that he was **Jesus the Christ.**

First Time Jesus Speaks
of His Death

From that time forth began Jesus to show unto his disciples, how that he must go unto Jerusalem, and be rejected of the elders and suffer many things of chief priests and scribes, and be killed, and be raised again the third day.

Then Peter took him, and began to rebuke him, saying, Be it far from thee, Lord: this shall not be unto thee. But he turned and said unto **Peter, Get thee behind me, Satan: thou art an offence unto me: for thou savourest not the things that be of God, but those that be of men.**

Then said Jesus unto his disciples, **If any man will come after me, let him deny himself, and take up his cross daily and follow me. For what does a man profited, if he shall gain the whole world, and lose himself and be cast away, or what shall a man give in exchange for his soul? For whosoever shall be ashamed of me and of my words, of him shall the Son of man be ashamed, when he shall come in his own glory and in his Father and of the holy angels. But I tell you of a truth, there be some standing here, which shall not taste of death, till they see the Son of man coming in his kingdom.**

Jesus is Transfigured

And after six days Jesus taketh Peter, James, and John his brother, and leadeth them up into an high mountain apart by themselves: And as he prayed, Peter and they that were with him were heavy with sleep; and when they were awaken they saw his glory, and the fashion of his countenance was altered, and he was transfigured before them: and his face did shine as the sun, and his raiment was white as light, whiter than snow; so as no bleach could bleach them.

And, behold, there appeared unto them Moses and Elias: Who appeared in glory, and spake of his decease which he should accomplish at Jerusalem. But Peter answered and said unto Jesus, Lord, it is good for us to be here: if thou wilt, let us make here three tabernacles; one for thee, and one for Moses, and one for Elias. While he yet spake, behold, there came a cloud that overshadowed them: and voice came out of the cloud, saying, *This is my beloved Son, in whom I am well pleased; hear ye him.* And when the disciples heard it, they fell pond their faces and were sore afraid. And Jesus came and touched them, and said, **Arise, and be not afraid.** When they had lifted up their eyes, they saw no man, save Jesus only.

And as they came down from the mountain, he charged them that they should tell no man what things they had seen, till the Son of man has been risen from the dead. And they kept that saying with themselves questioning one with another; what the rising from the dead should mean. They asked him, saying why say the scribes that Elias must first come? And Jesus answered and said unto them, **Elias truly shall first come, and restore all things, and how it is written** of the Son of man, that he must suffer many things, and be set at nought. But I say unto you, That Elias is indeed come, and they have done unto him whatsoever they listed; Then the disciples understood that he spake unto them of John the Baptist.

Jesus Heals Demon-possessed Child

And it came to pass, that on the next day, when they were come down from the hill, he saw a great multitude, and he came unto them, and the scribes came questioning with them. When they beheld him, and were greatly amazed, saluting him. And he asked the scribes, **What question ye with them?** And one of the multitudes, a certain man, came kneeling down unto him, and saying, Master, I brought my son to thy disciples, and they could not cure him. So I have him brought unto thee, for he has hath a dumb spirit; for off times he falleth into the fire and into the water, to destroy him: And wheresoever he taketh him, he teareth him: and he foameth, at the mouth, an gnasheth with his teeth, and pineth away: Lord have mercy on my son, for he is my only son, if thou canst do any thing, have compassion on us, and help us.

O faithless and perverse generation, how long shall I be with you? How long shall I suffer you? Bring him hither to Me. And they brought him unto him: and when he saw him, straightway the spirit tare him; and he fell on the ground, and wallowed foaming at the mouth. And he asked his father, **How long is it ago since this came unto him?** And he said, of a child. Jesus said unto him, **If thou canst believe, all things are possible to him that believeth.** And straightway the father of the child cried out, and said with tears, Lord, I believe: help thou mine unbelief.

When Jesus saw that the people came running together, He rebuked the foul spirit, the devil, saying unto him, **Thou dumb and deaf spirit, I charge thee, come out of him, and enter no more into him.** And the spirit cried, and rent him sore, and came out of him:

and he was as one dead; insomuch that many said, He is dead. But Jesus took him by the hand, and lifted him up; and he arose. And when he was come into the house, his disciples came to Jesus apart privately and asked Him, Why could not we cast him out?

This kind can come forth by nothing, but by prayer and fasting, and because of your unbelief: for verily I say unto you, If ye have faith as a grain of mustard seed, ye shall say unto this mountain, Remove hence to yonder place; and it shall remove; and nothing shall be impossible unto you.

And they were all amazed at the mighty power of God. While they wondered every one at all things which Jesus did.

Second Time Jesus Predicts His Death

And they departed thence, and passed through Galilee; and they abode outside the city, he would not that any man should know it.

For he taught his disciples, and said unto them, **Let these sayings sink down into your ears: for the Son of man shall be delivered into the hands of men, and shall be betrayed. And they shall kill him, and after that he is killed, he shall rise the third day.**

But they understood not that saying, because it was hid from them, that they perceived it not: and they feared to ask him of that saying, and they became exceeding sorry.

Peter Finds Coin in Fish's Mouth

And when they were come to Capernaum, they that received tribute money came to Peter, and said, Doth not your master pay tribute? He saith, yes. And when he was come into the house, Jesus prevented him, saying, **What thinkest thou, Simon? of whom do the kings of the earth take custom or tribute? of their own children, or of strangers?** Peter saith unto him, of strangers. Jesus said unto him, **Then are the children free. Notwithstanding, lest we should offend them, go thou to the sea, and cast an hook, and take up the fish that first cometh up; and when thou hast opened his mouth, thou shalt find a piece of money: that take, and give unto them for me and thee.**

The Disciples Argue Who would be the Greatest

And they came to Capernaum: being in the house came the disciples unto Jesus, he asked them, **What was it that ye disputed among yourselves by the way?** But they held their peace: for by the way they had disputed among themselves, who should be the greatest. And he sat down, and called the twelve, and saith unto them, **If any man desire to be first, the same shall be last of all, and servant of all.** And he called a little child unto him, took and set him in the midst of them: and when he had taken him in his arms he said unto them, **Verily I say unto you, Except ye be converted, and become as this little child, Ye shall not enter into the kingdom of heaven.**

Whosoever therefore shall humble himself as this little child, the same is greatest in the kingdom of heaven. Whosoever shall receive one of such children in my name receiveth me; and whosoever shall receive me, receiveth not me, but him that sent me. And whosoever shall offend one of these little ones which believe in me, it were better for him that a millstone were hanged about his neck, and that he were drowned in the depth of the sea.

Disciples Forbid Another To Use Jesus's Name

Then John ask him, saying, Master, we saw one casting out devils in thy name, And because he followeth not us: so we forbad him.

But Jesus said, **Forbid him not: for there is no man which shall do a miracle in my name, that can lightly speak evil of me. For he that is not against us is for us.**

For whosoever shall give you a cup of water to drink in my name, because ye belong to Christ, verily I say unto you, he shall not lose his reward.

Warns against Temptation

Woe unto the world because of offences! For it must needs be that offences come; but woe to that man by whom the offence cometh. Therefore if thy hand or thy foot offend thee, cut them off, and cast them from thee: it is better for thee to enter into life halt or maimed, rather than having two hands or two feet to be cast into everlasting fire. And if thine eye offend thee, pluck it out, and cast it from thee: it is better for thee to enter into life with one eye, rather than having two eyes to be cast into hell fire.

Jesus Warns against Looking Down on Others

Take heed that ye despise not one of these little ones; for I say unto you, That in heaven their angels do always behold the face of my Father which is in heaven. For the Son of man is come to save that which was lost. How think ye? if a man have an hundred sheep, and one of them be gone astray, doth he not leave the ninety nine and goeth into the mountains, and seeketh that which is gone astray? And if so be that he find it, verily I say unto you, he rejoiceth more of that sheep, than of the ninety nine which went not astray. Even so it is not the will of your Father which is in heaven, that one of these little ones should perish.

Teaches How to Treat A Believer Who Sins

Moreover if thy brother shall trespass against thee, go and tell him his fault between thee and him alone: if he shall hear thee, thou hast gained thy brother. But if he will not hear thee, then take with thee one or two more, that in the mouth of two or three witnesses every word may be established. And if he shall neglect to hear them, tell it unto the church: but if he neglect to hear the church, let him be unto thee as an heathen man and a publican.

Verily I say unto you, What soever ye shall bind on earth shall be bound in heaven: and whatsoever ye shall loose on earth shall be loosed in heaven. Again I say unto you, That if two of you shall agree on earth as touching any thing that they shall ask, it shall be done for them of my Father which is in heaven. For where two or three are gathered together in my name, there am I in the midst of them.

Unforgiving Debtor

Then came Peter to him, and said, Lord, how oft shall my brother sin against me, and I forgive him? till seven times? Jesus saith unto him, **I say not unto thee, until seven times: but, until seventy times seven. Therefore is the kingdom of heaven likened unto a certain king, which would take account of his servants. And when he had begun to reckon, one was brought unto him, which owed him ten thousand talents. But forasmuch as he had not to pay, his lord commanded him to be sold, and his wife, and children, and all that he had, for payment to be made. The servant therefore fell down; and worshiped him, saying, Lord, have patience with me, and I will pay thee all. Then the lord of that servant was moved with compassion, and loosed him, and forgave him the debt. But the same servant went out, and found one of his fellow servants, which owed him an hundred pence: and he laid hands on him, and took him by the throat, saying, Pay me that thou owest.**

And his fellow servant fell down at his feet, and besought him, saying, Have patience with me, and I will pay thee all. And he would not: but went and cast him into prison, till he should pay the debt. So when his fellow servants saw what was done, they were very sorry, and came and told unto their lord all that was done. Then his lord, after that he had called him, said unto him, O thou wicked servant, I forgave thee all that debt, because thou desiredst of me: Shouldest not thou also have had compassion on thy fellow servant, even as I had pity on thee? And his lord was wroth, and delivered him to the tormentors, till he should pay

all that was due unto him. So likewise shall my heavenly Father do also unto you; if ye from your hearts forgive not every one his brother their trespasses.

Jesus's Brothers Ridicule Him

After these things Jesus walked in Galilee: for he would not walk in Jewry, because the Jews sought to kill him. Now the Jew's feast of tabernacles was at hand. His brethren therefore said unto him, Depart hence, and go into Judaea, that thy disciples also may see the works that thou doest. For there is no man that doeth any thing in secret, and he himself seeketh to be known openly. If thou do these things, show thyself to the world. For neither did his brethren believe in him.

Then Jesus said unto them, **My time is not yet come: but your time is always ready. The world cannot hate you; but me it hateth, because I testify of it, that the works thereof are evil. Go ye up unto this feast: I go not up yet unto this feast; for my time is not yet full come**. When he had said these words unto them, he abode still in Galilee.

The Cost of Following Jesus Christ

Now when Jesus saw the great multitudes about him, He gave commandment to depart unto the other side of the lake.

And a certain scribe came, and said unto him, Master: I will follow thee whithersoever thou goest. And Jesus saith unto him, **The foxes have holes, and the birds of the air have nests; but the Son of man hath nowhere to lay his head.** And another of his disciples said unto him, Lord, suffer me first to go and bury my father. **But Jesus said unto him, Follow me; and let the dead bury their dead: but go thou and preach the kingdom of God.** And another also said, Lord, I will follow thee; but let me first go bid them farewell, which are at home at my house. And Jesus said unto him, **No man, having put his hand to the plough, and looking back, is fit for the kingdom of God.**

And it came to pass, when the time was come that he should be received up, he steadfastly set his face to go to Jerusalem, and sent messengers before his face: and they went, and entered into a village of the Samaritans, to make ready for him. And they did not receive him, because He was as though he would go to Jerusalem. And when his disciples James and John saw this, they said, Lord, wilt thou that we command fire to come down from heaven, and consume them, even as Elias did? But he turned, and rebuked them, and said, **Ye know not what manner of spirit ye are of. For the Son of man is not come to destroy men's lives, but to save them.**

Jesus Teaches Openly at the Temple

But when his brethren were gone up, then went he also up unto the feast, not openly, but as it were in secret. Then the Jews sought him at the feast, and said, Where is he? And there was much murmuring among the people concerning him: for some said, He is a good man: others said, Nay; but he deceiveth the people. Howbeit no man spake openly of him for fear of the Jews. Now about the midst of the feast Jesus went up into the temple, and taught. And the Jews marvelled, saying: How knoweth this man these sayings, having never learned?

Jesus answered them, and said, **My doctrine is not mine, but his that sent me. If any man will do his will, he shall know of the doctrine, whether it be of God, or whether I speak of myself. He that speaketh of himself seeketh his own glory: but he that seeketh his glory that sent him, the same is true, and no unrighteousness is in him. Did not Moses give you the law, and yet none of you keepeth the law? Why go ye about to kill me?** The people answered and said, Thou hast a devil: who goeth about to kill thee?

Jesus answered and said unto them, **I have done one work, and ye all marvel. Moses therefore gave unto you circumcision; (not because it is of Moses, but of the Fathers;) and ye on the sabbath day circumcise a man. If a man on the sabbath day receive circumcision, that the law of Moses should not be broken; are ye angry at me, because I have made a man whole on the sabbath day? Judge not according to the appearance, but judge righteous judgment.**

Then said some of them of Jerusalem, Is not this he, whom they seek to kill? But, lo, he speaketh boldly, and they say nothing unto him. Do the rulers know indeed that this is the very Christ? Howbeit we know this man whence he is: but when Christ cometh, no man knoweth whence he is. Then cried Jesus in the temple as he taught, saying, **Ye both know me, and ye know whence I am: and I am not come of myself, but he that sent me is true, whom ye know not. But I know him: for I am from him, and he hath sent me.** Then they sought to take him: but no man laid hands on him, because his hour was not yet come. And many of the people believed on him, and said, When Christ cometh, will he do more miracles than these which this man hath done?

Religious Leaders Attempt to Arrest Jesus

The Pharisees heard that the people murmured such things concerning him; and the Pharisees and the chief priests sent officers to take him. Then said Jesus unto them, **Yet a little while am I with you, and then I go unto him that sent me. Ye shall seek me, and shall not find me: and where I am, thither ye cannot come.** Then said the Jews among themselves, Whither will he go, that we shall not find him? will he go unto the dispersed among the Gentiles, and teach the Gentiles? What manner of saying is this that he hath said, Ye shall seek me, and shall not find me: and where I am, thither ye cannot come?

In the last day, that great day of the feast, Jesus stood and cried, saying, **If any man thirst, let him come unto me, and drink. He that believeth on me, as the scripture hath said, out of his belly shall flow rivers of living water.** (But this spake he of the Spirit, which they that believe on him should receive: for the *Holy Ghost* was not yet *given*; because that Jesus was not yet glorified.)

Many of the people therefore, when they heard this saying, said, Of a truth this is the Prophet. Others said, This is the Christ. But some said, Shall Christ come out of Galilee? Hath not the scripture said, That Christ cometh of the seed of David, and out of the town of Bethlehem, where David was?

So there was a division among the people because of him. And some of them would have taken him; but no man laid hands on him. Then came the officers to the chief priests and Pharisees; and they said unto them, Why have ye not brought him? The officers answered,

Never man spake like this man. Then answered them the Pharisees, Are ye also deceived? Have any of the rulers or of the Pharisees believed on him? But this people who knoweth not the law are cursed. Nicodemus saith unto them, (he that came to Jesus by night, being one of them,) Doth our law judge any man, before it hear him, and know what he doeth? They answered and said unto him, Art thou also of Galilee? Search, and look: for out of Galilee ariseth no prophet. And every man went unto his own house.

JESUS FORGIVES ADULTEROUS WOMAN

Jesus went unto the mount of Olives. And early in the morning he came again into the temple, and all the people came unto him; and he sat down, and taught them. And the scribes and Pharisees brought unto him a woman taken in adultery; and when they had set her in the midst, They said unto him, Master, this woman was taken in adultery, in the very act. Now Moses in the law commanded us, that such should be stoned: but what sayest thou? This they said, tempting him, that they might have to accuse him. But Jesus stooped down, and with his finger wrote on the ground, *as though he heard them not.*

So when they continued asking him, he lifted up himself, and said unto them, **He that is without sin among you, let him first cast a stone at her.** And again he stooped down, and wrote on the ground. And they which heard *it*, being convicted by their own conscience, went out one by one, beginning at the eldest, even unto the last: and Jesus was left alone, and the woman standing in the midst. When Jesus had lifted up himself, and saw none but the woman, he said unto her, **Woman, where are those thine accusers? hath no man condemned thee?** She said, No man, Lord. And **Jesus said unto her, Neither do I condemn thee: go, and sin no more.**

Jesus is the Light of the World

Then spake Jesus again unto them, saying, **I am the light of the world: he that followeth me shall not walk in darkness, but shall have the light of life.** The Pharisees therefore said unto him, Thou bearest record of thyself; thy record is not true. Jesus answered and said unto them, **Though I bear record of myself, yet my record is true: for I know whence I came, and whither I go; but ye cannot tell whence I come, and whither I go. Ye judge after the flesh; I judge no man. And yet if I judge, my judgment is true: for I am not alone, but I and the Father that sent me. It is also written in your law, that the testimony of two men is true. I am one that bear witness of myself, and the Father that sent me beareth witness of me.** Then said they unto him, Where is thy Father? **Jesus answered, Ye neither know me, nor my Father: if ye had known me, ye should have known my Father also.** These words spake Jesus in the treasury, as he taught in the temple: and no man laid hands on him; for his hour was not yet come.

Jesus Warns of Coming Judgment

Then said Jesus again unto them, **I go my way, and ye shall seek me, and shall die in your sins: whither I go, ye cannot come.** Then said the Jews, Will he kill himself? because he saith, Whither I go, ye cannot come. And he said unto them, **Ye are from beneath; I am from above: ye are of this world; I am not of this world. I said therefore unto you, that ye shall die in your sins: for if ye believe not that I am he, ye shall die in your sins**. Then said they unto him, Who art thou? And Jesus saith unto them, **Even the same that I said unto you from the beginning. I have many things to say and to judge of you: but he that sent me is true; and I speak to the world those things which I have heard of him.** They understood not that he spake to them of the Father. Then said Jesus unto them, **When ye have lifted up the Son of man, then shall ye know that I am he, and that I do nothing of myself; but as my Father hath taught me, I speak these things. And he that sent me is with me: the Father hath not left me alone; for I do always those things that please him**. As he spake these words, many believed on him.

Jesus Speaks About God's True Children

Then said Jesus to those Jews which believed on him, **If ye continue in my word, then are ye my disciples indeed; And ye shall know the truth, and the truth shall make you free**. They answered him, we be Abraham's seed, and were never in bondage to any man: how sayest thou, Ye shall be made free?

Jesus answered them, **Verily, verily, I say unto you, Whosoever committeth sin is the servant of sin. And the servant abideth not in the house for ever: but the Son abideth ever. If the Son therefore shall make you free, ye shall be free indeed. I know that ye are Abraham's seed; but ye seek to kill me, because my word hath no place in you. I speak that which I have seen with my Father: and ye do that which ye have seen with your father**. They answered and said unto him, Abraham is our father. Jesus saith unto them, **If ye were Abraham's children, ye would do the works of Abraham. But now ye seek to kill me, a man that hath told you the truth, which I have heard of God: this did not Abraham. Ye do the deeds of your father**.

Then said they to him, we be not born of fornication; we have one Father, even God. Jesus said unto them, **If God were your Father, ye would love me: for I proceeded forth and came from God; neither came I of myself, but he sent me. Why do ye not understand my speech? even because ye cannot hear my word. Ye are of your father the devil, and the lusts of your father ye will do. He was a murderer from the beginning, and abode not in the truth, because there is** no truth in him. When he speaketh a lie, he speaketh of his own: for he is a liar, and the father of it. And because I tell you the truth, ye believe me not. Which of you convinceth me of sin? And if I say the truth, why do ye not believe me? He that is of God heareth God's words: ye therefore hear them not, because ye are not of God.

Jesus States He Is Eternal

Then answered the Jews, and said unto him, Say we not well that thou art a Samaritan, and hast a devil? Jesus answered, **I have not a devil; but I honor my Father, and ye do dishonor me. And I seek not mine own glory: there is one that seeketh and judgeth. Verily, verily, I say unto you, If a man keep my saying, he shall never see death.** Then said the Jews unto him, Now we know that thou hast a devil. Abraham is dead, and the prophets; and thou sayest, If a man keepth my saying, he shall never taste of death. Art thou greater than our father Abraham, which is dead? and the prophets are dead: whom makest thou thyself?

Jesus answered, **If I honor myself, my honor is nothing: it is my Father that honoreth me; of whom ye say, that he is your God: Yet ye have not known him; but I know him: and if I should say, I know him not, I shall be a liar like unto you: but I know him, and keep his saying. Your father Abraham rejoiced to see my day: and he saw it, and was glad.** Then said the Jews unto him, Thou art not yet fifty years old, and hast thou seen Abraham? Jesus said unto them, **Verily, verily, I say unto you, Before Abraham was, I am.** Then took they up stones to cast at him: but Jesus hid himself, and went out of the temple, going through the midst of them, and so passed by.

Jesus Sends Out the Seventy

After these things the Lord appointed other seventy also, and sent them two by two before his face into every city and place, whither he himself would come. Therefore said he unto them, **The harvest truly is great, but the labourers are few: pray ye therefore the Lord of the harvest, that he would send forth labourers into his harvest. Go your ways: behold, I send you forth as lambs among wolves. Carry neither purse, nor scrip, nor shoes: and salute no man by the way. And into whatsoever house ye enter, first say, Peace be to this house. And if the son of peace be there, your peace shall rest upon it: if not, it shall turn to you again. And in the same house remain, eating and drinking such things as they give: for the labourer is worthy of his hire. Go not from house to house. And into whatsoever city ye enter, and they receive you, eat such things as are set before you: And heal the sick that are therein, and say unto them, The kingdom of God is come nigh unto you.**

But into whatsoever city ye enter, and they receive you not, go your ways out into the streets of the same, and say, Even the very dust of your city, which cleaveth on us, we do wipe off against you: notwithstanding be ye sure of this, that the kingdom of God is come nigh unto you. But I say unto you, that it shall be more tolerable in that day for Sodom, than for that city. Woe unto thee, Chorazin! woe unto thee, Bethsaida! for if the mighty works had been done in Tyre and Sidon, which have been done in you, they had a great while ago repented, sitting in sackcloth and ashes. But it shall be more tolerable for Tyre and Sidon at the judgment, than for you. And thou, Capernaum, which art exalted to heaven, shalt be thrust down to hell. He that heareth you heareth me; and he that despiseth you despiseth me; and he that despiseth me despiseth him that sent me.

The Seventy Messengers Return

And the seventy returned again with joy, saying, Lord, even the devils are subject unto us through thy name. And he said unto them, **I beheld Satan as lightning fall from heaven. Behold, I give unto you power to tread on serpents and scorpions, and over all the power of the enemy: and nothing shall by any means hurt you. Notwithstanding in this rejoice not, that the spirits are subject unto you; but rather rejoice, because your names are written in heaven.** In that hour Jesus rejoiced in spirit, and said, **I thank thee, O Father, Lord of heaven and earth, that thou hast hid these things from the wise and prudent, and hast revealed them unto babes: even so, Father; for so it seemed good in thy sight. All things are delivered unto me of my Father: and no man knoweth who the Son is, but the Father; and who the Father is, but the Son, and he to whom the Son will reveal him.** And he turned him unto his disciples, and said privately, **Blessed are the eyes which see the things that ye see: For I tell you, that many prophets and kings have desired to see those things which ye see, and have not seen them; and to hear those things which ye hear, and have not heard them.**

Jesus Tells Parable of Good Samaritan

And, behold, a certain lawyer stood up, and tempted him, saying, Master, what shall I do to inherit eternal life? He said unto him, **What is written in the law? how readest thou?** And he answering said, Thou shalt love the Lord thy God with all thy heart, and with all thy soul, and with all thy strength, and with all thy mind; and thy neighbor as thyself. And he said unto him, **Thou hast answered right: this do, and thou shalt live.** But he, willing to justify himself, said unto Jesus, And who is my neighbor? And Jesus answering said, **A certain man went down from Jerusalem to Jericho, and fell among thieves, which stripped him of his raiment, and wounded him, and departed, leaving him half dead. And by chance there came down a certain priest that way: and when he saw him, he passed by on the other side. And likewise a Levite, when he was at the place, came and looked upon him, and passed by on the other side. But a certain Samaritan, as he journeyed, came where he was: and when he saw him, he had compassion on him, and went to him, and bound up his wounds, pouring in oil and wine, and set him on his own beast, and brought him to an inn, and took care of him. And on the morrow when he departed, he took out two pence, and gave them to the host, and said unto him, Take care of him; and whatsoever thou spendest more, when I come again, I will repay thee. Which now of these three, thinkest thou, was neighbor unto him that fell among the thieves?** And he said, He that showed mercy on him. Then said Jesus unto him, **Go, and do thou likewise.**

Jesus Visits Mary and Martha

Now it came to pass, as they went, that he entered into a certain village: and a certain woman named Martha received him into her house. And she had a sister called Mary, which also sat at Jesus' feet, and heard his word. But Martha was cumbered about much serving, and came to him, and said, Lord, dost thou not care that my sister hath left me to serve alone? bid her therefore that she help me. And Jesus answered and said unto her, **Martha, Martha, thou art careful and troubled about many things: But one thing is needful: and Mary hath chosen that good part, which shall not be taken away from her.**

Jesus Teaches His Disciples about Prayer

And it came to pass, that, as he was praying in a certain place, one of his disciples came said unto him, Lord, teach us to pray, as John also taught his disciples. And he said unto them, When ye pray, say, ***Our Father which art in heaven, Hallowed be thy name. Thy kingdom come. Thy will be done, as in heaven, so in earth. Give us day by day our daily bread. And forgive us our sins; for we also forgive every one that is indebted to us. And lead us not into temptation; but deliver us from evil.*** And he said unto them, **Which of you shall have a friend, and shall go unto him at midnight, and say unto him, Friend, lend me three loaves; For a friend of mine in his journey is come to me, and I have nothing to set before him? And he from within shall answer and say, Trouble me not: the door is now shut, and my children are with me in bed; I cannot rise and give thee. I say unto you, Though he will not rise and give him, because he is his friend, yet because of his persistents he will rise and give him as many as he needeth. And I say unto you, Ask, and it shall be given you; seek, and ye shall find; knock, and it shall be opened unto you. For every one that asketh receiveth; and he that seeketh findeth; and to him that knocketh it shall be opened. If a son shall ask bread of any of you that is a father, will he give him a stone? or if he ask a fish, will he for a fish give him a serpent? Or if he shall ask an egg, will he offer him a scorpion? If ye then, being evil, know how to give good gifts unto your children: how much more shall your heavenly Father give the Holy Spirit to them that ask him?**

JESUS ANSWERS HOSTILE ACCUSATIONS

And he was casting out a devil, and it was dumb. And it came to pass, when the devil was gone out, the dumb spake; and the people wondered. But some of them said, He casteth out devils through Beelzebub the chief of the devils. And others, tempting *him*, sought of him a sign from heaven. But he, knowing their thoughts, said unto them, **Every kingdom divided against itself is brought to desolation; and a house divided against a house falleth. If Satan also be divided against himself, how shall his kingdom stand? because ye say that I cast out devils through Beelzebub. And if I by Beelzebub cast out devils, by whom do your sons cast them out? therefore shall they be your judges. But if I with the finger of God cast out devils, no doubt the kingdom of God is come upon you.**

When a strong man armed keepeth his palace, his goods are in peace: But when a stronger than he shall come upon him, and overcome him, he taketh from him all his armour wherein he trusted, and divideth his spoils. He that is not with me is against me: and he that gathereth not with me scattereth. When the unclean spirit is gone out of a man, he walketh through dry places, seeking rest; and finding none, he saith, I will return unto my house whence I came out. And when he cometh, he findeth it swept and garnished. Then goeth he, and taketh to him seven other spirits more wicked than himself; and they enter in, and dwell there: and the last state of that man is worse than the first.

And it came to pass, as he spake these things, a certain woman of the company lifted up her voice, and said unto him, blessed is the womb that bare thee, and the paps which thou hast sucked. But he said, **Yea rather, blessed are they that hear the word of God, and keep it.**

Jesus Warns against Unbelief

And when the people were gathered thick together, he began to say, **This is an evil generation: they seek a sign; and there shall no sign be given it, but the sign of Jonas the prophet. For as Jonas was a sign unto the Ninevites, so shall also the Son of man be to this generation. The queen of the south shall rise up in the judgment with the men of this generation, and condemn them: for she came from the utmost parts of the earth to hear the wisdom of Solomon; and, behold, a greater than Solomon is here. The men of Nineve shall rise up in the judgment with this generation, and shall condemn it: for they repented at the preaching of Jonas; and, behold, a greater than Jonas is here.**

Jesus Teaches About the Light Within

No man, when he hath lighted a candle, putteth it in a secret place, neither under a bushel, but on a candlestick, that they which come in may see the light. The light of the body is the eye: therefore when thine eye is single, thy whole body also is full of light; but when thine eye is evil, thy body also is full of darkness. Take heed therefore that the light which is in thee be not darkness. If thy whole body therefore be full of light, having no part dark, the whole shall be full of light, as when the bright shining of a candle doth give thee light.

Jesus Speaks against Religious Leaders

And as he spake, a certain Pharisee besought him to dine with him: and he went in, and sat down to meat. And when the Pharisee saw *it*, he marvelled that he had not first washed before dinner. And the Lord said unto him, **Now do ye Pharisees make clean the outside of the cup and the platter; but your inward part is full of ravening and wickedness. Ye fools, did not he that made that which is without make that which is within also? But rather give alms of such things as ye have; and, behold, all things are clean unto you. But woe unto you, Pharisees! for ye tithe mint and rue and all manner of herbs, and pass over judgment and the love of God: these ought ye to have done, and not to leave the other undone. Woe unto you, Pharisees! for ye love the uppermost seats in the synagogues, and greetings in the markets. Woe unto you, scribes and Pharisees, hypocrites! for ye are as graves which appear not, and the men that walk over them are not aware of them.** Then answered one of the lawyers, and said unto him, Master, thus thy saying thou reproachest us also.

And he said, **Woe unto you also, ye lawyers! for ye lade men with burdens grievous to be borne, and ye yourselves touch not the burdens with one of your fingers. Woe unto you! for ye build the sepulchres of the prophets, and your fathers killed them. Truly ye bear witness that ye allow the deeds of your fathers: for they indeed killed them. Therefore also said the wisdom of God, I will send them prophets and apostles, and some of them they shall** slay and persecute: That the blood of all the prophets, which was shed from the foundation of the world, may be required of this generation; From the blood of Abel unto the blood of Zacharias, which perished between the altar and the temple: verily I say unto you, It shall be required of this generation. Woe unto you, lawyers! for ye have taken away the key of knowledge: ye entered not in yourselves, and them that were entering in ye hindered. And as he said these things unto them, the scribes and the Pharisees began to urge him vehemently, and to provoke him to speak of many things: Laying wait for him, and seeking to catch something out of his mouth, that they might accuse him.

Jesus Speaks Against Hypocrisy

In the meantime, when there were gathered together an innumerable multitude of people, insomuch that they troden one upon another, he began to say unto his disciples first of all, **Beware ye of the leaven of the Pharisees, which is hypocrisy. For there is nothing covered, that shall not be revealed; neither hid, that shall not be known. Therefore whatsoever ye have spoken in darkness shall be heard in the light; and that which ye have spoken in the ear in closets shall be proclaimed upon the housetops. And I say unto you my friends, Be not afraid of them that kill the body, and after that have no more that they can do. But I will forewarn you whom ye shall fear: Fear him, which after he hath killed hath power to cast into hell; yea, I say unto you, Fear him. Are not five sparrows sold for two farthings, and not one of them is forgotten before God? But even the very hairs of your head are all numbered. Fear not therefore: ye are of more value than many sparrows.**

Also I say unto you, Whosoever shall confess me before men, him shall the Son of man also confess before the angels of God: But he that denieth me before men shall be denied before the angels of God. And whosoever shall speak a word against the Son of man, it shall be forgiven him: but unto him that blasphemeth against the Holy Ghost it shall not be forgiven. And when they bring you unto the synagogues, and unto magistrates, and powers, take ye no thought how or what thing ye shall answer, or what ye shall say: For the Holy Ghost shall teach you in the same hour what ye ought to say.

Parable of the Rich Fool

And one of the company said unto him, Master, speak to my brother, that he divide the inheritance with me. And he said unto him, **Man, who made me a judge or a divider over you?** And he said unto them, **Take heed, and beware of covetousness: for a man's life consisteth not in the abundance of the things which he possesseth.** And he spake a parable unto them, saying, **The ground of a certain rich man brought forth plentifully: and he thought within himself, saying, What shall I do, because I have no room where to bestow my fruits? And he said, This will I do: I will pull down my barns, and build greater; and there will I bestow all my fruits and my goods. And I will say to my soul, Soul, thou hast much goods laid up for many years; take thine ease, eat, drink, and be merry. But God said unto him, Thou fool, this night thy soul shall be required of thee: then whose shall those things be, which thou hast provided? So is he that layeth up treasure for himself, and is not rich toward God.**

Warns about Worry

And he said unto his disciples, **Therefore I say unto you, take no thought for your life, what ye shall eat; neither for the body, what ye shall put on. The** life is more than meat, and the body is more than raiment. Consider the ravens: for they neither sow nor reap; which neither have storehouse nor barn; and God feedeth them: how much more are ye better than the fowls? And which of you with taking thought can add to his stature one cubit? If ye then be not able to do that thing which is least, why take ye thought for the rest? Consider the lilies how they grow: they toil not, they spin not; and yet I say unto you, that Solomon in all his glory was not arrayed like one of these. If then God so clothe the grass, which is to day in the field, and tomorrow is cast into the oven; how much more will he clothe you, O ye of little faith? And seek not ye what ye shall eat, or what ye shall drink, neither be ye of doubtful mind. For all these things do the nations of the world seek after: and your Father knoweth that ye have need of these things.

But rather seek ye the kingdom of God; and all these things shall be added unto you. Fear not, little flock; for it is your Father's good pleasure to give you the kingdom. Sell that ye have, and give alms; provide yourselves bags which wax not old, a treasure in the heavens that faileth not, where no thief approacheth, neither moth corrupteth. For where your treasure is, there will your heart be also.

Preparing for His Coming

Let your loins be girded about, and your lights burning; And ye yourselves like unto men that wait for their lord, when he will return from the wedding; that when he cometh and knocketh, they may open unto him immediately. Blessed are those servants, whom the lord when he cometh shall find watching: verily I say unto you, that he shall gird himself, and make them to sit down to meat, and will come forth and serve them. And if he shall come in the second watch, or come in the third watch, and find them so, blessed are those servants. And this know, that if the goodman of the house had known what hour the thief would come, he would have watched, and not have suffered his house to be broken through. Be ye therefore ready also: for the Son of man cometh at an hour when ye think not.

Jesus teaches about Coming Division

I am come to send fire upon the earth; and what will I, if it be already kindled? But I have a baptism to be baptized with; and how am I straitened till it be accomplished! Suppose ye that I am come to give peace on earth? I tell you, Nay; but rather division: For from henceforth there shall be five in one house divided, three against two, and two against three. The father shall be divided against the son, and the son against the father; the mother against the daughter, and the daughter against the mother; the mother in law against her daughter in law, and the daughter in law against her mother in law.

Jesus Warns About the Future Crisis

And he said also to the people, **When ye see a cloud rise out of the west, straightway ye say, There cometh a shower; and so it is. And when ye see the south wind blow, ye say, There will be heat; and it cometh to pass. Ye hypocrites, ye can discern the face of the sky and of the earth; but how is it that ye do not discern this time?**

Yea, and why even of yourselves judge ye not what is right? When thou goest with thine adversary to the magistrate, as thou art in the way, give diligence that thou mayest be delivered from him; lest he hale thee to the judge, and the judge deliver thee to the officer, and the officer cast thee into prison.

I tell thee, thou shalt not depart thence, till thou hast paid the very last mite.

Jesus Calls People to Repent

There were present at that season some who told Him about the Galileans whose blood Pilate had mingled with their sacrifices. And Jesus answered and said unto them, **"Do you suppose that these Galileans were worse sinners than all other Galileans, because they suffered such things? I tell ye, no; but unless ye repent you will all likewise perish. Or those eighteen on whom the tower in Siloam fell and killed them, do ye think that they were worse sinners than all other men who dwelt in Jerusalem? I tell you, no; but unless ye repent you will all likewise perish."**

He also spake this parable: **"A certain man had a fig tree planted in his vineyard, and he came seeking fruit on it and found none. Then he said to the keeper of his vineyard, 'Look, for three years I have come seeking fruit on this fig tree and findth none. Cut it down; why doeth it use up the ground?' But he answered and said unto him, 'Sir, let it alone this year also, until I dig around it and fertilize it. And if it bears fruit, well. But if not, after that ye can cut it down.'"**

Jesus Heals a Handicapped Woman

Now He was teaching in one of the synagogues on the Sabbath. And behold, there was a woman who had a spirit of infirmity eighteen years, and was bent over and could in no way raise herself up. But when Jesus saw her, He called *her un*to *Him* and said to her, **"Woman, you are loosed from your infirmity."** And He laid *His* hands upon her, and immediately she was made straight, and glorified God. But the ruler of the synagogue answered with indignation, because Jesus had healed on the Sabbath; and he said unto the crowd, "There are six days on which men ought to work; therefore come and be healed on them, and not on the Sabbath day." The Lord then answered him and said, **"Hypocrite! Does not each one of you on the Sabbath loose his ox or donkey from the stall, and lead it away to water it? So ought not this woman, being a daughter of Abraham, whom Satan has bound Lo, these eighteen years, be loosed from this bond on the Sabbath?"** And when he had said these things, all His adversaries were put to shame; and all the multitude rejoiced for all the glorious things that were done by Him.

Jesus Teaches About the Kingdom of God

Then He said, "What is the kingdom of God like? And to what shall I compare it? It is like a mustard seed, which a man took and planth in his garden; and it grew and became a large tree, and the birds of the air nested in its branches." And again He said, "To what shall I liken the kingdom of God? It is like leaven, which a woman took and hid in three measures of meal till it was all leavened."

Jesus Heals the Man Who Was Born Blind

Now as *Jesus* passed by, He saw a man who was blind from birth. And His disciples asked Him, saying, "Rabbi, who sinned, this man or his parents, that he was born blind?" **Jesus answered, "Neither this man nor his parents sinned, but that the works of God should be revealed in him. I must work the works of Him who sent Me while it is day; the night is coming when no one can workth. As long as I am in the world, I am the light of the world."** When He had said these things, He spat on the ground and made clay with the saliva; and He anointed the eyes of the blind man with the clay. And He said unto him, **"Go, wash in the pool of Siloam"** (which is translated, Sent). So he went and washed, and came back seeing. Therefore the neighbors and those who previously had seen that he was blind said, "Is not this he who sat and begged?" Some said, "This is he." Others said, "He is like him." He said, "I am *he*."

Religious Leaders Question
Blind Man

Therefore they said unto him, "How were your eyes opened?" He answered and said, "A Man called Jesus made clay and anointed my eyes and said unto me, 'Go to the pool of Siloam and wash.' So I went and washed, and I received my sight." Then they said unto him, "Where is He?" He said, "I do not know."

They brought him who formerly was blind to the Pharisees. Now it was a Sabbath when Jesus made the clay, and opened his eyes. Then the Pharisees also asked of him again how he had received his sight. He said unto them, "He put clay on my eyes, and I washed, and I see." Therefore some of the Pharisees said, "This Man is not from God, because He does not keep the Sabbath." Others said, "How can a man who is a sinner do such signs?" And there was a division among them.

They said unto the blind man again, "What do you say about Him because He opened your eyes?" He saidth, "He is a prophet." But the Jews did not believe concerning him, that he had been blind and received his sight, until they called the parents of him who had received his sight. And they asked them, saying, "Is this your son, who ye say was born blind? How then does he now see?"

His parents answered them and said, "We know that this is our son, and that he was born blind; but by what means he now seeth we do not know, or who opened his eyes, we know not. He is of age; ask him. He will speak for himself." His parents said these things because they feared the Jews, for the Jews had agreed already that if anyone confessed that He was Christ, he would be put out of the synagogue. Therefore his parents said, "He is of age; ask him."

So they again called the man who was blind, and said unto him, "Give God the glory! We know that this Man is a sinner." He answered and said, "Whether He is a sinner or not I do not know. One thing I know: that though I was blind, now I see." Then they said unto him again, "What did He do to you? How did He openth your eyes?" He answered them, "I told you already, and you did not listen. Why do you want to hear *it* again? Do you also want to become His disciples?" Then they reviled him and said, "Ye are His disciple, but we are Moses' disciples. We know that God spake to Moses; *as for* this *fellow*, we know not where He is from."

The man answered and said unto them, "Why, this is a marvelous thing, that ye do not know where He is from; yet He has opened my eyes! Now we know that God does not hear sinners; but if anyone is a worshiper of God and does His will, He hears him. Since the world began it has been unheard of that anyone openth the eyes of one who was born blind. If this Man were not from God, He could do nothing." They answered and said unto him, "You were completely born in sins, and are ye teaching us?" And they cast him out.

Jesus Teaches About Spiritual Blindness

Jesus heard that they had cast him out; and when He had found him, He said unto him, **"Do you believe in the Son of God?"** He answered and said, "Who is He, Lord, that I may believeth in Him?" And Jesus said unto him, **"You have both seen Him and it is He who is talking with you."** Then he said, "Lord, I believe!" And he worshiped Him.

And Jesus said, **"For judgment I have come into this world, that those who do not see may see, and that those who say they see may be made blind."**

Then some of the Pharisees who were with Him heard these words, and said unto Him, "Are we so blind also?" Jesus said unto them, **"If ye were blind, you would have no sin; but now you say, 'We see.' Therefore your sin remains.**

Jesus Is the Good Shepherd

Verily, verily, I say unto you, He that entereth not by the door into the sheepfold, but climbeth up some other way, the same is a thief and a robber. But he that entereth in by the door is the shepherd of the sheep. To him the porter openeth; and the sheep hear his voice: and he calleth his own sheep by name, and leadeth them out. And when he putteth forth his own sheep, he goeth before them, and the sheep follow him: for they know his voice. And a stranger will they not follow, but will flee from him: for they know not the voice of strangers. This parable spake Jesus unto them: but they understood not what things they were which he spake unto them.

Then said Jesus unto them again, **Verily, verily, I say unto you, I am the door of the sheep. All that ever came before me are thieves and robbers: but the sheep did not hear them. I am the door: by me if any man enter in, he shall be saved, and shall go in and out, and find pasture. The thief cometh not, but for to steal, and to kill, and to destroy: I am come that they might have life, and that they might have it more abundantly. I am the good shepherd: the good shepherd giveth his life for the sheep. But he that is an hireling, and not the shepherd, whose own the sheep are not, seeth the wolf coming, and leaveth the sheep, and fleeth: and the wolf catcheth them, and scattereth the sheep. The hireling fleeth, because he is an hireling, and careth not for the sheep. I am the good shepherd, and know my sheep, and am known of mine. As the Father knoweth me, even so know I the Father: and I lay down my life for the sheep. And other sheep I have, which are not of** this fold: them also I must bring, and they shall hear my voice; and there shall be one fold, and one shepherd. Therefore doth my Father love me, because I lay down my life, that I might take it again. No man taketh it from me, but I lay it down of myself. I have power to lay it down, and I have power to take it again. This commandment have I received of my Father. There was a division therefore again among the Jews for these sayings. And many of them said, He hath a devil, and is mad; why hear ye him? Others said, These are not the words of him that hath a devil. Can a devil open the eyes of the blind?

Religious Leaders Surround Jesus at the Temple

And it was at Jerusalem the feast of the dedication, and it was winter. And Jesus walked in the temple in Solomon's porch. Then came the Jews round about him, and said unto him, How long dost thou make us to doubt? If thou be the Christ, tell us plainly. Jesus answered them, **I told you, and ye believed not: the works that I do in my Father's name, they bear witness of me. But ye believe not, because ye are not of my sheep, as I said unto you. My sheep hear my voice, and I know them, and they follow me: And I give unto them eternal life; and they shall never perish, neither shall any man pluck them out of my hand. My Father, which gave them me, is greater than all; and no man is able to pluck them out of my Father's hand. I and my Father are one.** Then the Jews took up stones again to stone him. Jesus answered them, **Many good works have I showed you from my Father; for which of those works do ye stone me?**

The Jews answered him, saying, For a good work we stone thee not; but for blasphemy; and because that thou, being a man, makest thyself God. Jesus answered them, **Is it not written in your law, I said, Ye are gods? If he called them gods, unto whom the word of God came, and the scripture cannot be broken; Say ye of him, whom the Father hath sanctified, and sent into the world, Thou blasphemest; because I said, I am the Son of God? If I do not the works of my Father, believe me not. But if I do, though ye believe not me, believe the works: that ye may know, and believe, that the Father is in me, and I in him.** Therefore they sought again to take him: but he escaped out of their hand, and went away again beyond Jordan into the place where John at first baptized; and there he abode. And many resorted unto him, and said, John did no miracle: but all things that John spake of this man were true. And many believed on him there.

Jesus Teaches about Entering the Kingdom

And He went through the cities and villages, teaching, and journeying toward Jerusalem. Then one spake unto Him, "Lord, are there few who are saved?"

And He said unto him, **"Strive to enter through the narrow gate, for many, I say unto you, will seek to enter in and will not be able. When once the Master of the house has risen up and shut the door, and ye begin to standth outside and knock at the door, saying, 'Lord, Lord, open for us,' and He will answer and say unto you, 'I know ye not where you are from,' then ye will begin to say, 'We ate and drank in Your presence, and thou hast taught in our streets.' But He shall say, 'I know ye not or where you are from. Depart from Me, all ye workers of iniquity.' Where there shell be weeping and gnashing of teeth, when ye shell see Abraham, and Isaac, and Jacob, and all the prophets in the kingdom of God, and ye yourselves thrust out. And they will come from the east, and the west, from the north, and the south, and shall sit down in the kingdom of God. And indeed there are last who will be first, and there are first which shall will be last."**

On that very day some Pharisees came, saying to Him, "Get out and depart from here, for Herod wants to kill You." And He said unto them, **"Go, tell that fox, 'Behold, I cast out demons and perform cures today and tomorrow, and the third day I shall be** perfected.' Nevertheless I must journey today, tomorrow, and the day following; for it shall not be that a prophet should perish outside of Jerusalem.

Jesus Grieves over Jerusalem

"O Jerusalem, Jerusalem, the one who killth the prophets and stones those who are sent to her! How often I wanted to gather your children together, as a hen gatherth her brood under her wings, but you were not willing! See! Your house is left to you desolate; and assuredly, I say unto you, ye shall not see Me until the time comes when ye say, 'Blessed is He who comes in the name of the Lord!'"

Jesus Heals Man with Dropsy

And it came to pass, as he went into the house of one of the chief Pharisees to eat bread on the sabbath day, that they watched him. And, behold, there was a certain man before him which had the dropsy. And Jesus answering spake unto the lawyers and Pharisees, saying, **Is it lawful to heal on the sabbath day?** And they held their peace. And he took *him*, and healed him, and let him go; and answered them, saying, **Which of you shall have an ass or an ox fallen into a pit, and will not straightway pull him out on the sabbath day? And they could not answer him again to these things.**

Jesus Teaches About Seeking Honor

And he put forth a parable to those which were bidden, when he marked how they chose out the chief rooms; saying unto them, **When thou art bidden of any man to a wedding, sit not down in the highest room; lest a more honorable man than thou be bidden of him; And he that bade thee and him come and say to thee, Give this man place; and thou begin with shame to take the lowest room. But when thou art bidden, go and sit down in the lowest room; that when he that bade thee cometh, he may say unto thee, Friend, go up higher: then shalt thou have worship in the presence of them that sit at meat with thee. For whosoever exalteth himself shall be abased; and he that humbleth himself shall be exalted.** Then said he also to him that bade him, **When thou makest a dinner or a supper, call not thy friends, nor thy brethren, neither thy kinsmen, nor thy rich neighbors; lest they also bid thee again, and a recompense be made thee. But when thou makest a feast, call the poor, the maimed, the lame, the blind: And thou shalt be blessed; for they cannot recompense thee: for thou shalt be recompensed at the resurrection of the just.** And when one of them that sat at meat with him heard these things, he said unto him, Blessed *is* he that shall eat bread in the kingdom of God.

Jesus Tells Parable
Of the Great Feast

Then said he unto him, **a certain man made a great supper, and bade many: And sent his servant at supper time to say to them that were bidden, Come; for all things are now ready. And they all with one consent began to make excuse. The first said unto him, I have bought a piece of ground, and I must needs go and see it: I pray thee have me excused. And another said, I have bought five yoke of oxen, and I go to prove them: I pray thee have me excused. And another said, I have married a wife, and therefore I cannot come. So that servant came, and showed his lord these things. Then the master of the house being angry said to his servant, Go out quickly into the streets and lanes of the city, and bring in hither the poor, and the maimed, and the halt, and the blind. And the servant said, Lord, it is done as thou hast commanded, and yet there is room. And the lord said unto the servant, Go out into the highways and hedges, and compel them to come in, that my house may be filled. For I say unto you, That none of those men which were bidden shall taste of my supper.**

The Cost of Being a Disciple

And there went great multitudes with him: and he turned, and said unto them, **If any man come to me, and hate not his father, and mother, and wife, and children, and brethren, and sisters, yea, and his own life also, he cannot be my disciple. And whosoever doth not bear his cross, and come after me, cannot be my disciple. For which of you, intending to build a tower, sitteth not down first, and counteth the cost, whether he have sufficient to finish it? Lest haply, after he hath laid the foundation, and is not able to finish it, all that behold it begin to mock him, Saying, This man began to build, and was not able to finish. Or what king, going to make war against another king, sitteth not down first, and consulteth whether he be able with ten thousand to meet him that cometh against him with twenty thousand? Or else, while the other is yet a great way off, he sendeth an ambassage, and desireth conditions of pcacc. So likewise, whosoever he be of you that forsaketh not all that he hath, he cannot be my disciple. Salt is good: but if the salt have lost his savour, wherewith shall it be seasoned? It is neither fit for the land, nor yet for the dunghill; but men cast it out. He that hath ears to hear, let him hear.**

Parable of the Lost Sheep

Then drew near unto him all the publicans and sinners for to hear him. And the Pharisees and scribes murmured, saying, This man receiveth sinners, and eateth with them. And he spake this parable unto them, saying, **What man of you, having an hundred sheep, if he lose one of them, doth not leave the ninety and nine in the wilderness, and go after that which is lost, until he find it? And when he hath found it, he layeth it on his shoulders, rejoicing. And when he cometh home, he calleth together his friends and neighbors, saying unto them, Rejoice with me; for I have found my sheep which was lost. I say unto you, that likewise joy shall be in heaven over one sinner that repenteth, more than over ninety and nine just persons, which need no repentance.**

Parable of Lost Coin

Either what woman having ten pieces of silver, if she lose one piece, doth not light a candle, and sweep the house, and seek diligently till she find it? And when she hath found it, she calleth her friends and her neighbors together, saying, Rejoice with me; for I have found the piece which I had lost. Likewise, I say unto you, there is joy in the presence of the angels of God over one sinner that repenteth.

Parable of Lost Son

And he said, **a certain man had two sons:** And the younger of them said to his father, Father, give me the portion of goods that falleth to me. And he divided unto them his living. And not many days after the younger son gathered all together, and took his journey into a far country, and there wasted his substance with riotous living. And when he had spent all, there arose a mighty famine in that land; and he began to be in want. And he went and joined himself to a citizen of that country; and he sent him into his fields to feed swine. And he would fain have filled his belly with the husks that the swine did eat: and no man gave unto him. And when he came to himself, he said, How many hired servants of my Father's have bread enough and to spare, and I perish with hunger! I will arise and go to my father, and will say unto him, Father, I have sinned against heaven, and before thee, and am no more worthy to be called thy son: make me as one of thy hired servants.

And he arose, and came to his father. But when he was yet a great way off, his father saw him, and had compassion, and ran, and fell on his neck, and kissed him. And the son said unto him, Father, I have sinned against heaven, and in thy sight, and am no more worthy to be called thy son. But the father said to his servants, Bring forth the best robe, and put it on him; and put a ring on his hand, and shoes on his feet: And bring hither the fatted calf, and kill it; and let us eat, and be merry: For this my son was dead, and is alive again; he was lost, and is found. And they began to be merry. Now his elder son was in the field: and as he came and drew nigh to the house, he heard music and dancing. And he called one of the servants, and asked what these things meant. And he said unto him, Thy brother is come; and thy father hath killed the fatted calf, because he hath received him safe and sound. And he was angry, and would not go in: therefore came his father out, and intreated him. And he answering said to his father, Lo, these many years do I serve thee, neither transgressed I at any time thy commandment: and yet thou never gavest me a kid, that I might make merry with my friends: But as soon as this thy son was come, which hath devoured thy living with harlots, thou hast killed for him the fatted calf. And he said unto him, Son, thou art ever with me, and all that I have is thine. It was meet that we should make merry, and be glad: for this thy brother was dead, and is alive again; and was lost, and is found.

Jesus Tells the Parable Of the Shrewd Accountant

He also said to His disciples: **"There was a certain rich man who had a steward, and an accusation was brought to him that this man was wasting his goods. So he called him and said to him, 'What is this I hear about you? Give an account of your stewardship, for you can no longer be steward.'** **"Then the steward said within himself, 'What shall I do? For my master is taking the stewardship away from me. I cannot dig; I am ashamed to beg. I have resolved what to do, that when I am put out of the stewardship, they may receive me into their houses.'**

"So he called every one of his master's debtors to him, and said to the first, 'How much do you owe my master?' And he said, 'A hundred measures of oil.' So he said to him, 'Take your bill, and sit down quickly and write fifty.' Then he said to another, 'And how much do you owe?' So he said, 'A hundred measures of wheat.' And he said to him, 'Take your bill, and write eighty.' So the master commended the unjust steward because he had dealt shrewdly. For the sons of this world are more shrewd in their generation than the sons of light.

"And I say to you, make friends for yourselves by unrighteous mammon, that when you fail, they may receive you into an everlasting home. He who is faithful in what is least is faithful also in much; and he who is unjust in what is least is unjust also in much. Therefore if you have not been faithful in the unrighteous mammon, who will commit to your trust the true riches? And if

you have not been faithful in what is another man's, who will give you what is your own?

"No servant can serve two masters; for either he will hate the one and love the other, or else he will be loyal to the one and despise the other. **You cannot serve God and mammon.**"

Now the Pharisees, who were lovers of money, also heard all these things, and they derided Him. And He said to them, "**You are those who justify yourselves before men, but God knows your hearts.**

For what is highly esteemed among men is an abomination in the sight of God. "The law and the prophets were until John. Since that time the kingdom of God has been preached, and everyone is pressing into it. And it is easier for heaven and earth to pass away than for one tittle of the law to fail. "Whoever divorces his wife and marries another commits adultery; and whoever marries her who is divorced from her husband commits adultery.

Jesus Tells about the Beggar And the Rich Man

"There was a certain rich man who was clothed in purple and fine linen and fared sumptuously every day. But there was a certain beggar named Lazarus, full of sores, who was laid at his gate, desiring to be fed with the crumbs which fell from the rich man's table. Moreover the dogs came and licked his sores. So it was that the beggar died, and was carried by the angels to Abraham's bosom. The rich man also died and was buried. And being in torments in Hades, he lifted up his eyes and saw Abraham afar off, and Lazarus in his bosom. "Then he cried and said, 'Father Abraham, have mercy on me, and send Lazarus that he may dip the tip of his finger in water and cool my tongue; for I am tormented in this flame.' But Abraham said, 'Son, remember that in your lifetime you received your good things, and likewise Lazarus evil things; but now he is comforted and you are tormented. And besides all this, between us and you there is a great gulf fixed, so that those who want to pass from here to you cannot, nor can those from there pass to us.'

"Then he said, 'I beg you therefore, father, that you would send him to my father's house, for I have five brothers, that he may testify to them, lest they also come to this place of torment.' Abraham said to him, 'They have Moses and the prophets; let them hear them.' And he said, 'No, father Abraham; but if one goes to them from the dead, they will repent.' But he said to him, 'If they do not hear Moses and the prophets, neither will they be persuaded though one rise from the dead.'"

Jesus Tells about Forgiveness and Faith

Then He said to the disciples, **"It is impossible that no offenses should come, but woe to him through whom they do come! It would be better for him if a millstone were hung about his neck, and he were thrown into the sea, than that he should offend one of these little ones. Take heed to yourselves. If your brother sins against you, rebuke him; and if he repents, forgive him. And if he sin's against you seven times in a day, and seven times in a day returns unto you, saying, 'I repent,' ye shall forgive him."** And the apostles said unto the Lord, "Increase our faith."

So the Lord said, **"If ye have faith as a mustard seed, you can say unto this mulberry tree, 'Be pulled up by the roots and be planted in the sea,' and it would obey you. And which of ye, having a servant plowing or tending sheep, will say unto him when he has come in from the field, 'Come at once and sit down to eat'? But will he not rather say unto him, 'Prepare something for my supper, and gird yourself and serve me till I have eaten and drank, and afterward ye will eat and drink'? Does he think that servant because he didth the things that were commanded of him? I think not. So likewise ye, when you have done all those things which ye are commanded, say, 'We are unprofitable servants. We have done what was our duty to do.'"**

LAZARUS BECOMES SICK AND DIES

Now a certain man was sick, named Lazarus, of Bethany, the town of Mary and her sister Martha. (It was that Mary which anointed the Lord with ointment, and wiped his feet with her hair, whose brother Lazarus was sick.) Therefore his sisters sent unto him, saying, Lord, behold, he whom thou lovest is sick. When he had heard therefore that he was sick, he said, **This sickness is not unto death, but for the glory of God, that the Son of God might be glorified thereby.** Now Jesus loved Martha, and her sister, and Lazarus. But he abode two days still in the same place where he was. Then after that saith he unto *his* disciples, Let us go into Judaea again. *His* disciples said unto him, Master, the Jews of late sought to stone thee; and goest thou thither again? Jesus answered, **Are there not twelve hours in the day? If any man walk in the day, he stumbleth not, because he seeth the light of this world. But if a man walk in the night, he stumbleth, because there is no light in him.** These things said he: and after that he saith unto them, **Our friend Lazarus sleepeth; but I go, that I may awake him out of sleep.** Then said his disciples, Lord, if he sleep, he shall do well. Howbeit Jesus spake of his death: but they thought that he had spoken of taking of rest in sleep. Then said Jesus unto them plainly, **Lazarus is dead. And I am glad for your sakes that I was not there, to the intent ye may believe; nevertheless let us go unto him.** Then said Thomas, which is called Didymus, unto his fellow disciples, let us also go, that we may die with him.

Jesus Comforts Mary and Martha

Then when Jesus came, he found that he had lain in the grave four days already. Now Bethany was nigh unto Jerusalem, about fifteen furlongs off: And many of the Jews came to Martha and Mary, to comfort them concerning their brother. Then Martha, as soon as she heard that Jesus was coming, went and met him: but Mary sat still in the house. Then said Martha unto Jesus, *Lord*, if thou hadst been here, my brother had not died. But I know, that even now, whatsoever thou wilt ask of God, God will give *it* thee. Jesus saith unto her, **Thy brother shall rise again.** Martha saith unto him, I know that he shall rise again in the resurrection at the last day. Jesus said unto her, **I am the resurrection, and the life: he that believeth in me, though he were dead, yet shall he live: And whosoever liveth and believeth in me shall never die. Believest thou this?** She saith unto him, Yea, *Lord:* I believe that thou art the ***Christ, the Son of God***, which should come into the world. And when she had so said, she went her way, and called Mary her sister secretly, saying, The Master is come, and calleth for thee. As soon as she heard *that*, she arose quickly, and came unto him.

Now Jesus was not yet come into the town, but was in that place where Martha met him. The Jews then which were with her in the house, and comforted her, when they saw Mary, that she rose up hastily and went out, followed her, saying, She goeth unto the grave to weep there. Then when Mary was come where Jesus was, and saw him, she fell down at his feet, saying unto him, *Lord*, if thou hadst been here, my brother had not died. When Jesus therefore saw her weeping, and the Jews also weeping which came with her, he groaned in the spirit, and was troubled, and said, **Where have ye laid him?** They said unto him, Lord, come and see. *"Jesus wept".*

Then said the Jews, Behold how he loved him! And some of them said, Could not this man, which opened the eyes of the blind, have caused that even this man should not have died?

Jesus Raises Lazarus From the Dead

Jesus therefore again groaning within himself he cometh to the grave. It was a cave, and a stone lay upon it. Jesus said, **Take ye away the stone.** Martha, the sister of him that was dead, saith unto him, Lord, by this time he stinketh: for he hath been dead four days. **Jesus saith unto her, Said I not unto thee, that, if thou wouldest believe, thou shouldest see the glory of God?** Then they took away the stone from the place where the dead was laid. And Jesus lifted up his eyes, and said, **Father, I thank thee that thou hast heard me. And I know that thou hearest me always: but because of the people which stand by I said it, that they may believe that thou hast sent me.** And when he thus had spoken, he cried with a loud voice, *Lazarus, come forth.* And he that was dead came forth, bound hand and foot with graveclothes: and his face was bound about with a napkin. Jesus saith unto them, Loose him, and let him go.

Religious Leaders Plot to Kill Jesus

Then many of the Jews which came to Mary, and had seen the things which Jesus did, believed on him. But some of them went their ways to the Pharisees, and told them what things Jesus had done. Then gathered a council of chief priests and the Pharisees and said, What do we? for this man doeth many miracles. If we let him thus alone, all men will believe on him: and the Romans shall come and take away both our place and nation. And one of them, named Caiaphas, being the high priest that same year, saith unto them, Ye know nothing at all, Nor consider that it is expedient for us, that one man should die for the people, and that the whole nation perish not. And this spake he not of himself: but being high priest that year, he prophesied that Jesus should die for that nation; And not for that nation only, but that also he should gatherth together in one the children of God that were scattered abroad. Then from that day forth they took counsel together for to put him to death. Jesus therefore walked no more openly among the Jews; but went thence unto a country near to the wilderness, into a city called Ephraim, and there continued with his disciples. And the Jews' passover was nigh at hand: and many went out of the country up to Jerusalem before the passover, to purify themselves. Then sought they for Jesus, and spake among themselves, as they stood in the temple, What think ye, that he will not come to the feast? Now both the chief priests and the Pharisees had given a commandment, that, if any man knew where he were, he should show *it*, that they might take him.

Jesus Heals Ten Lepers

And it came to pass, as he went to Jerusalem, that he passed through the midst of Samaria and Galilee. And as he entered into a certain village, there met him ten men that were lepers, which stood afar off: And they lifted up their voices, and said, Jesus, Master, have mercy on us. And when he saw *them*, he said unto them, **Go show yourselves unto the priests.**

And it came to pass, that, as they went, they were cleansed. And one of them, when he saw that he was healed, turned back, and with a loud voice glorified God, and fell down on his face at his feet, giving him thanks: and he was a Samaritan. And Jesus answering said, **Were there not ten cleansed? but where are the nine? There are not found that returned to give glory to God, save this stranger.** And he said unto him, **Arise, go thy way: thy faith hath made thee whole.**

Then Shall the Kingdom of God Come

And when he was demanded of the Pharisees, when the kingdom of God should come, he answered them and said, **The kingdom of God cometh not with observation: Neither shall they say, Lo here! or, lo there! for, behold, the kingdom of God is within you.** Then He said unto the disciples, **"The days will come when you will desire to see one of the days of the Son of Man, and you will not see it. And they will say unto you, 'Look here!' or 'Look there!' Do not go after them or follow them. For as the lightning that flashes out of one part under heaven shines to the other part under heaven, so also the Son of Man will be in His day. But first He must suffer many things and be rejected by this generation. And as it was in the days of Noah, so shall it be also in the days of the Son of Man: They ate, they drank, they married wives, they were given in marriage, until the day that Noah entered the ark, and the flood came and destroyed them all. Likewise as it was also in the days of Lot: They ate, they drank, they bought, they sold, they planted, they built; but on the day that Lot went out of Sodom it rained fire and brimstone from heaven and destroyed them all. Even so will it be in the day when the Son of Man is revealed.**

"In that day, he who is on the housetop, and his goods are with in, let him not come down to take them away. And likewise the one who is in the field, let him not turn back. Remember Lot's wife. Whoever seeks to save his life will lose it, and whoever loses his life will preserve it. I tell you, in that night there will be two in one

bed: the one will be taken and the other will be left. Two women will be grinding together: the one will be taken and the other left. Two men will be in the field: the one will be taken and the other left." And they answered and said unto Him, **"Where, Lord?"** So He said to them, **"Wherever the body is, there the eagles will be gathered together."**

Parable of the Persistent Widow

Then He spoke a parable unto them, that men always ought to pray and not lose heart, saying: **"There was in a certain city a judge who did not fear God nor regard man. Now there was a widow in that city; and she came unto him, saying, 'Get justice for me from my adversary.' And he would not for a while; but afterward he said within himself, 'Though I do not fear God nor regard man, yet because this widow troublth me I will avenge her, lest by her continual coming she weary me.'"**

Then the Lord said, **"Hear what the unjust judge saith. And shall God not avenge His own elect who cry out day and night unto Him, though He bears long with them? I tell you that He will avenge them speedily. Nevertheless, when the Son of Man comes, will He really find faith on the earth?"**

Parable of Two Men Who Prayed

Also He spoke this parable to some who trusted in themselves that they were righteous, and despised others: **"Two men went up to the temple to pray, one a Pharisee and the other a tax collector. The Pharisee stood and prayed thus with himself, 'God, I thank You that I am not like other men—extortioners, unjust, adulterers, or even as this tax collector. I fast twice a week; I give tithes of all that I possess.' And the tax collector, standing afar off, would not so much as raise his eyes to heaven, but beat his breast, saying, 'God, be merciful to me a sinner!' I tell you, this man went down to his house justified rather than the other; for everyone who exalts himself will be humbled, and he who humbles himself will be exalted."**

Jesus Teaches about Marriage and Divorce

When Jesus had finished these sayings he arose from thence, and cometh into the coasts beyond the Jordan; And the multitudes followed him; and he was wanted, and healed them and taught them.

And the Pharisees also came unto him, and asked him. Is it lawful for a man to put away his wife? Tempting him. **Have ye not read, what Moses command you?** They said, Moses suffered to write a bill of divorcement, and to put her away. Then Jesus answered and said unto them, **For the hardness of your heart he wrote you this precept. But from the beginning of the creation God made them male and female. For this cause shall a man leave his father and mother, and cleave to his wife; And they twain shall be one flesh: so then they are no more twain but one flesh. What therefore God hath joined together, let not man put asunder. And I say unto you, Whosoever shall put away his wife except for fornication, (or as to say unfaithfulness) and shall marry another committeth adultery: and whoso marrieth her which is put away doth commit adultery.**

And as they were in the house his disciples asked of him again the matter. If be the case, of the man be so with his wife, it is not good to marry. But he said unto them, **Not all men can receive this saying, save they to whom it is given. For there are some eunuchs, which were so born from their mother's womb: and there are some which were made eunuchs of men: and there be eunuchs, which have make themselves eunuchs for the kingdom of heaven's sake. He that is able let him receive it.**

Jesus Blesses Little Children

Then were brought unto him young little children, that he should put his hands on them, and pray: but then the disciples rebuked those that brought them. But when Jesus saw it, he was much displeased, and called them unto him, and said, **Suffer the little children to come unto me, and forbid them not: for of such is the kingdom of God. Verily I say unto you, Whosoever shall not receive the kingdom of God as a little child, he shall in no wise enter there in. And he took them up in his arms, put his hands upon them, and blessed them, and departed thence.**

Jesus Speaks To Rich Young Man

And when he was gone forth into the way, there came running unto him a certain ruler, and kneeling down before him, asking him, saying, Good Master, what good thing shall I do, that I may inherit eternal life? **Why callest thou me good? There is none good but one, that is, God: but if thou willet enter into life, keep the commandments.** He saith unto him, Which? Jesus said, **Thou shalt do no murder, thou shalt not commit adultery, Thou shalt not steal, Thou shalt not bear false witness, Defraud not, Honor thy father and thy mother: and Thou shalt love thy neighbor as thyself.** And he answered and said unto him, Master, all these have I observed from my youth.

What lack I yet? Now when Jesus heard these things beholding him, loved him, he said; **If thou wilt be perfect, Yet lackest thou one thing: go sell all that thou hast and distribute unto the poor, and thou shalt have treasure in heaven: and come, take up the cross, and follow me.** And when he heard this, he was very sorrowful: for he was very rich. Saddened, he went away; Jesus knew how sorrowful, it made him, looked round about, and saith unto his disciples,

How hard is it for the rich
To enter the kingdom?

Verily I say unto you, **How hard shall it for they that have riches enter into the kingdom of heaven. And again I say unto you, It is easier for a camel to go through the eye of a needle, than for a rich man to enter into the kingdom of God.** Then his disciples heard it, they were exceedingly amazed, saying, Who then can be saved? But Jesus beheld them, and said unto them, **With men this is impossible; but with God all things are possible.** Then answered Peter and said unto him, Behold, we have forsaken all, and followed thee; what therefore shall we have? And Jesus said unto them, **Verily I say unto you, That ye which have followed me, in the regeneration when the Son of man shall sit on the throne of is glory, ye also shall sit upon twelve thrones, judging the twelve tribes of Israel. Verily I say unto you, There is no man that hath left house, or brethren, or sisters, or father, or mother, or wife, or children, or lands, for my sake, and the gospel's, but he shall receive an hundredfold now in this time, and the time to come, houses, and brethren, and sisters, and mothers, and children, and lands, with persecutions; and in the world to come eternal life. But many that are first shall be last; and the last shall be first.**

PARABLE OF THE WORKERS PAID EQUALLY

"For the kingdom of heaven is like unto a landowner who went out early in the morning to hire laborers for his vineyard. Now when he had agreed with the laborers for a denarius a day, he sent them into his vineyard. And he went out about the third hour and saw others standing idle in the marketplace, and said unto them, 'Ye also go into the vineyard, and whatever is right I will give you.' So they went. Again he went out about the sixth and the ninth hour, and did likewise. And about the eleventh hour he went out and found others standing idle, and said unto them, 'Why have ye been standing here idle all day?' They said unto him, 'Because no one hired us.' He said to them, 'Ye also go into my vineyard, and whatever is right you will receive.'

"So when evening had come, the owner of the vineyard saith unto his steward, 'Call the laborers and give them their wages, beginning with the last to the first.' And when those came who were hired about the eleventh hour, they each received a denarius. But when the first came, they supposed that they would receive more; and they likewise received each a denarius.

And when they had received it, they complained against the landowner, saying, 'These last men have worked only one hour, and ye made them equal to us who have borne the burden and the heat of the day.' But he answered one of them and saith, 'Friend, I am doing you no wrong. Did ye not agree with me for a denarius? Take what is yours and go your way. I wish to give to this last man the same as unto you. Is it not lawful for me to do what I wish with my own things? Or is your eye evil because I am good?' So the last will be first, and the first last. For many are called, but few chosen."

Jesus's Third Prediction
Of His Death

And when they were in the way going up to Jerusalem; Jesus went beforeth them. And they were amazed; and as they followed, they were afraiten. And he took again the twelve, and began to tell them what things should happen unto him.

Behold, we go up to Jerusalem. And all things that are written by the prophets concerning the Son of man shall be accomplished. For he shall be delivered unto chief priests, and to the scribes; and they shall condemn him, and shall deliver him unto the Gentiles, and shall be mock, spat upon and spitefully entreated, and they shall scourge him, and put him to death, by crucifying, him and the third day he shall rise again. And they understood none of these things: and this saying was hid from them, neither knew they the things which were spoken.

Jesus Teaches About Serving Others

Then came to him the mother of Zebedees children, her two sons James and John, worshipping him, and desiring of him saying Master, would that thou shouldest do for my son's whatsoever I shall desire, And he said unto her. **What would ye that I should do for you?** She said unto him, Grant that these my two sons may sit, the one on thy right hand, and the other on the left, in thy kingdom. But Jesus said unto her**, Ye know not what ye ask. Are ye able to drink of the cup that I shall drink of, and to be baptized with the baptism that I am baptized with?** They said unto him, we are able. And he saith unto them, **Ye shall indeed drink of the cup that I drink of; and with the baptism that I am baptized with shall ye be baptized: But to sit on my right hand and on my left hand is not mine to give; but it shall be given to them for whom it is prepared of my father.**

And when the ten heard them they were moved with indignation against the two brethren and began to be much displeased with James and John. But Jesus called them to him, and saith unto them, **Ye know that the princes of the Gentiles exercise dominion over them, and they that are great exercise authority upon them. But it shall not be so among you: but whosoever will be great among you, let him be your minister; And whosoever will be chief among you, let him be your servant: Even as the Son of man came not to be ministered unto, but to minister, and to give his life a ransom for many.**

Jesus Heals Blind Beggar

And they came unto Jericho: and as he went out of Jericho with his disciples and a great number of people, a blind beggar whose name was Bartimaeus, the son of Timaeus, and his blind friend, sat by the highway side, crying out begging. And when they heard that it was Jesus of Nazareth, they called out to him, *"Jesus,"* Son of David have mercy upon us. But they which went before him, charged them and rebuked them that they should hold their peace: but they crieth out the more, Jesus Thou Son of David have mercy on us. Then Jesus heard, He stood and commanded that they have them brought unto him. So they call the blind men, saying unto them, be of good comfort, rise; he calleth thee. And they cast away their garments, rose, and came unto Jesus. Then they came near, He asked of them, **What wilt thou that I should do unto you?** They said unto him, Lord, that our eyes may be opened. So Jesus had compassion upon them, and touched their eyes: and immediately their eyes received sight and they followed him, glorifying God; and all the people, when they saw it, gave praise unto God.

JESUS BRINGS SALVATION
TO ZACCHAEUS' HOUSE

Then *Jesus* entered and passed through Jericho. Now behold, there *was* a man named Zacchaeus who was a chief tax collector, and he was rich. And he sought to see who Jesus was, but could not because of the crowd, for he was of short stature. So he ran ahead and climbed up into a sycamore tree to see Him, for He was going to pass that way. And when Jesus came to the place, He looked up and saw him, and said unto him, **"Zacchaeus, make haste and come down, for today I must stay at thy house."** So he made haste and came down, and received Him joyfully. But when they saw *it,* they all complained, saying, "He has gone to be a guest with a man who is a sinner."

Then Zacchaeus stood and said unto the Lord, "Look, Lord, I giveth half of all my goods unto the poor; and if I have taken anything from anyone by false accusation, I restore fourfold." And Jesus saith unto him, **"Today salvation has come unto this house, because he also is a son of Abraham; for the Son of Man has come to seek and to save that which was lost."**

Parable of the Ten Servants

Now as they heard these things, He spake another parable, because He was near Jerusalem and because they thought the kingdom of God would appear immediately. Therefore He said unto them.

"A certain nobleman went into a far country to receive for himself a kingdom and to return. So he called three of his servants, delivered unto them ten minas, and said unto them, 'Do business till I comth.' But his citizens hated him, and sent a delegation after him, saying, 'We will not have this man to reign over us.'

"And so it was that when he returned, having received the kingdom, he then commanded those servants, to whom he had given the money, to be called unto him, that he might know how much every man had gained by trading. Then came the first, saying, 'Master, your mina has earned ten minas.' And he said unto him, 'Well done, good servant; because ye were faithful in a very little, have authority over ten cities.' And the second came, saying, 'Master, your mina has earned five minas.'

"Likewise he said unto him, 'You also be over five cities.' Then another came, saying, 'Master, here is your mina, which I have kept put away in a handkerchief. For I fearth you, because ye are an austere man. You collect what ye did not deposit, and reap what ye did not sow.' And he said unto him, 'Out of your own mouth I will judge you, ye wicked servant. You knew that I was an austere man, collecting what I did not deposit and reaping what I did not sow. Why then did you not put my money in the bank, that at my coming I might have collected it with interest?' "And he saith unto those who stood by, 'Take the mina from him, and give it unto him who has ten minas.' (But they said unto him, 'Master, he has ten minas.') 'For I say unto you, that to everyone who has will be given; and from him who does not have, even what he has will be taketh away from him. But bring here those enemies of mine, who did not want me to reign over them, and slayth them before me."

Woman Anoints Jesus with Perfume

Then Jesus six days before the Passover came to Bethany, where Lazarus was, which had been dead, whom he raised from the dead, and had supper in the house of Simon the leper.

Martha served: but Lazarus was one of them that sat at the table with him. Then took Mary a pound of precious ointment, in an alabaster box with spikenard very precious; and costly. Broke the box and poured it upon his head as he sat at meat. Then poured the remainder unto his feet anointing the feet of Jesus, and wiping them with her hair: and the house was filled with the odor of the ointment. But when his disciples saw it, they had indignation, within themselves, but Judas Iscariot, Simon's son, which should betray him, spake up saying unto what purpose is this waste? For it might have been sold for more than three hundred pence, and have been given unto the poor. This he said not that he cared for the poor; but because he was a thief, and had the money bag, and bare what which was put therein.

Why troubth ye the woman let her alone, for she hath wrought a good work upon me. For ye have the poor always with you; but me ye have not always, For when so ever ye will, ye may do them good: She hath done what she could: For against the day of my burial hath she kept this. Verily I say unto you, Where so ever this gospel shall be preached in the whole world there shall also this, that this woman hath done be told for a memorial of her.

Much of people of the Jews therefore knew that he was there: and they came not for Jesus, sake only, but that they might see Lazarus also, whom he raised from the dead. But the chief priests consulted that they might put Lazarus also to death; because that by reason of him many of the Jews went away and believed on Jesus.

Jesus Rides into Jerusalem on a Donkey

And when he had thus spoken, he went forth, unto Jerusalem, and were come to Bethphage, unto the mount of Olives, he sendeth forth two of his disciples, and saith unto them, **Go into the village over against you and straightway ye shall find an ass tied, and colt with her: whereon never a man sat; loose them; and bring them unto me. And if any man ask you, why do ye loose them? Say ye that the Lord hath need of them; and straightway he will send them.** All this was done, that it might be fulfilled which was spoken by the prophet, saying, *Tell ye the daughter of Zion, Behold, thy King cometh unto thee, meek, and sitting upon and, a colt the foal of an ass.*

And the disciples went, and did as Jesus commanded them, and found the ass and the colt tied by the door without in a place where two ways met; and certain of them that stood there said unto them, Why do ye losts the ass an her colt? And they said unto them even as Jesus had commanded: and they let them go. For they found even as he had said unto them. And they brought them unto Jesus, and took the colt and cast their garments on him; and Jesus sat upon it. And as they drew even now at the descent of the mount of Olives, the whole multitude of the disciples went before them, cutting branches of palm trees, casting them before him as well as their garments, and began crying and rejoicing and praising God with a loud voice for all the mighty works that they had seen;

Saying, Blessed be the King that cometh in the name of the Lord: Hosanna; in the highest, Blessed be the kingdom of our father David, that cometh in the name of the Lord, peace in heaven, and glory in the highest.

And some of the Pharisees from among the multitude said unto him, Master, rebuke thy disciples. And he answered and said unto them, **I tell ye that, if these should hold their peace, the stones would immediately cry out.**

And when he was come near, he beheld the city, and wept over it,

Saying, **If thou hadst known, even thou, at least in this thy day, the things which belong unto thy peace! but now they are hid from thine eyes. For the days shall come upon thee, that thine enemies shall cast a trench about thee, and compass thee round, and keep thee in on every side, and shall lay thee even with the ground, and thy children within; and they shall not leave in thee one stone upon another; because thou newest not the time of thy visitation.**

These things understood not his disciples at the first: but when Jesus was glorified, then remembered they that these things were written of him, and that they had done these things unto him. The people therefore that was with him when he called Lazarus out of his grave, and raised him from the dead, bare record. For this cause the people also met him, for that they heard that he had done this miracle. The Pharisees therefore said among themselves, Perceive ye how ye prevail nothing? behold, the world is gone after him.

Jesus Clears the Temple Again

And on the morrow, when they were come from Bethany, he was hungry: And seeing a fig tree afar off having leaves, he came, if haply he might find any thereon: and when he came to it, he found nothing but leaves: for the time of figs was not yet. And Jesus spake and said unto it, **May no man eat fruit of thee hereafter for ever.** And his disciples heard it.

And they came to Jerusalem: and Jesus went into the temple, and began to cast out them that sold and bought in the temple. And overthrew the tables of the moneychangers, and the seats of them that sold doves; and would not suffer that any man should carry any vessel through the temple. And he taught, saying unto them, Is it not written, **My house shall be called of all nations the house of prayer, But you have turned it into a den of thieves.**

The blind and the lame came to him in the temple; and he healed them. And the scribes and chief priests heard it, and saw the wonderful things that he did, and the children crying in the temple, and saying, Hosanna to the Son of David; they were sore displeased, and said unto him, Hearest thou what these say? And Jesus saith unto them, **Yea; have ye never read, Out of the mouth of babes and sucklings thou hast perfected praise?** And he left them, and went out of the city into Bethany; and he lodged there. Then they sought how they might destroy him: for they feared him, because all the people was astonished at his doctrine, But they could not find what they might do: for all the people were attentive to hear him.

Jesus Explains Why He Must Die

Now there were certain Greeks among those who came up to worship at the feast. Then they came to Philip, who was from Bethsaida of Galilee, and asked him, saying, "Sir, we wish to see Jesus." Philip came and told Andrew, and in turn Andrew and Philip told Jesus.

But Jesus answered them, saying, **"The hour has come that the Son of Man should be glorified. Most assuredly, I say to you, unless a grain of wheat falls into the ground and dies, it remains alone; but if it dies, it produces much grain. He who loves his life will lose it, and he who hates his life in this world will keep it for eternal life. If anyone serves Me, let him follow Me; and where I am, there My servant will be also. If anyone serves Me, him My Father will honor.**

"Now My soul is troubled, and what shall I say? 'Father, save Me from this hour'? But for this purpose I came to this hour. Father, glorify Your name." Then a voice came from heaven, saying, **"I have both glorified *it* and will glorify *it* again."** Therefore the people who stood by and heard *it* said that it had thundered. Others said, "An angel has spoken to Him."

Jesus answered and said, **"This voice did not come because of Me, but for your sake. Now is the judgment of this world; now the ruler of this world will be cast out. And I, if I am lifted up from the earth, will draw all peoples to Myself."** This He said, signifying by what death He would die. The people answered Him, "We have heard from the law that the Christ remains forever; and how *can* you say, 'The Son of Man must be lifted up'? Who is this Son of Man?"

Then Jesus said unto them, **"A little while longer the light is with you. Walk while you have the light, lest darkness overtake you; he who walks in darkness does not know where he is going. While you have the light, believe in the light, that you may become sons of light."** These things Jesus spoke, and departed, and was hidden from them.

MOST OF THE PEOPLE DO NOT BELIEVE IN JESUS

But although He had done so many signs before them, they did not believe in Him, that the word of Isaiah the prophet might be fulfilled, which he spake:

"Lord, who has believed our report?

And to whom has the arm of the Lord been revealed?" Therefore they could not believe, because Isaiah said again: *"He has blinded their eyes and hardened their hearts,*

Lest they should see with their eyes,

Lest they should understand with their hearts and turn, So that I should heal them."

These things Isaiah said when he saw His glory and spake of Him. Nevertheless even among the rulers many believed in Him, but because of the Pharisees they did not confess Him, lest they should be put out of the synagogue; for they loved the praise of men more than the praise of God.

Jesus Summarizes His Message

Then Jesus cried out and said, **"He who believes in Me, believes not in Me but in Him who sent Me. And he who sees Me sees Him who sent Me. I have come as a light into the world, that whoever believes in Me should not abide in darkness. And if anyone hears my words and does not believe, I do not judge him; for I did not come to judge the world but to save the world. He who rejects Me, and does not receive my words, has that which judges him— the "Word" that I have spoken will judge him in the last day. For I have not spoken on My own authority; but the Father who sent Me gave me a command, what I should say and what I should speak. And I know that His command is everlasting life. Therefore, whatever I speak, just as the Father has told Me, so I speak."**

Jesus Says Disciples can Pray for Anything

And in the morning, as they passed by, they saw the fig tree dried up from the roots. And peter calling to remembrance saith unto him, Master, behold, the fig tree which thou cursedst is withered away. And Jesus answering saith unto them, **Have faith in God. For verily I say unto you, that if ye have faith in God. And doubt not, in his heart, and shall believe that those things which he saith shall come to pass; Ye shall not only do this which is done to the fig tree, but also if ye shall say unto this mountain, Be thou removed, and be thou cast into the sea; it shall be done.**

Therefore I say unto you, what things so ever ye desire, when ye pray, believe that ye receive them, and ye shall have them. And when ye stand praying, forgive, if ye have ought against any: that your Father also which is in heaven may forgive you your trespasses. But if ye do not forgive, neither will your Father which is in heaven forgive your trespasses.

RELIGIOUS LEADERS CHALLENGE JESUS'S AUTHORITY

And it came to pass, that on one of those days, they came again to Jerusalem: and entered into the temple, and as he was walking in the temple, he stopped and began to teach the people preaching the gospel. The chief priests and the scribes and the elders, came unto him and spake up to him saying, By what authority doest thou these things and who gave thee this authority?

And he answered and said unto them, **I will also ask you one question, which if ye tell me, I will like wise tell you by what authority I do these things. The baptism of John, whence was it? From heaven, or of men?** And they reasoned with themselves, saying, if we shall say, from heaven; he will say unto us, Why did ye not then believe him? But if we shall say, of men, we fear the people, for all hold John as a prophet. And all the people will stone us: And they answered and said unto Jesus, We cannot tell. And he said unto them, **Neither tell I you by what authority I do these things.**

Parable of the Two Sons

"But what do ye think? A man had two sons, and he came to the first and said, 'Son, go, work today in my vineyard.' He answered and saith, 'I will not,' but afterward he regretted it and went. Then he came to the second and said likewise. And he answered and saith, 'I go, sir,' but he did not go. Which of the two did the will of his father?"

They said unto Him, "The first."

Jesus said unto them, **"Assuredly, I say unto you that tax collectors and harlots enter the kingdom of God before you. For John came unto you in the way of righteousness, and ye did not believe him; but tax collectors and harlots did believed him; and when you saw it, ye did not afterward relent and believe."**

Parable about Wicked Farmers

Then began he to speak to the people this parable; **There was a certain householder, which planted a vineyard, and built up a hedged round about it, and dug a winepress in it, and built a tower, and let out to tenants, and went into a far country for a long time. And when the season drew near, for the fruit to be gathered, he sent his servant to the tenants that he might receive the fruits of the vineyard. But they caught him and beat him and sent him away empty.**

So he then sent forth three other servants, but they also seize them beat one, killed another, and stoned another, and sent them away empty handed. And again he sent unto them other servants but they cast stones, at them and wounded them on the head, handling them shamefully and sent them away. But last of all he sent unto them his well beloved son, his only son, saying they will reverence my son. But when the tenants saw the son, they said among themselves, This is the heir: come, let us kill him, and let us seize unto his inheritance. And they caught him, and killed him, and cast him out of the vineyard. What then will the lord of the vineyard do? He will come and destroy the wicked tenants, and will give the vineyard unto others, which shall render him the fruits in their seasons.

Jesus saith unto them, did ye never read in the scriptures, The stone which the builders rejected, the same is become the head of the corner: This the Lords doing, and it is marvelous in our eyes? Therefore I say unto you, kingdom of God shall be taken from

you, and given unto a nation bringing forth the fruits thereof. And whosoever shall fall on this stone shall be broken: but on whomsoever it shall fall, it will grind him to powder. And when the chief priests and Pharisees had heard his parables they perceived that he spake of them. But when they sought to lay hands on him, they feared the multitude, because they took him for a prophet. This was Lords doing, and it is marvelous in our eyes.

Parable of the Wedding Fest

And Jesus answered and spoke unto them again by parables and said: "The kingdom of heaven is like a certain king who arranged a marriage for his son, and sent out his servants to call those who were invited unto the wedding; and they were not willing to come. Again, he sent out other servants, saying, 'Tell those who are invited, "See, I have prepared my dinner; my oxen and fatted cattle are killed, and all things are ready. Come to the wedding."' But they made light of it and went their ways, one to his own farm, another unto his business. And the rest seized his servants, treated them spitefully, and killed them. But when the king heard about it, he was furious. And he sent out his armies, to destroyed those murderers, and burned up their city. Then he said to his servants, 'The wedding is ready, but those who were invited were not worthy. Therefore go into the highways, and as many as you find, invite unto the wedding.' So those servants went out into the highways and gathered together all whom they found, both bad and good. And the wedding hall was filled with guests.

"But when the king came in to see the guests, he saw a man there who did not have on a wedding garment. So he said unto him, 'Friend, how did ye come in here without a wedding garment?' And he was speechless. Then the king saith unto the servants, 'Bind him hand and foot, take him away, and cast him into outer darkness; there will be weeping and gnashing of teeth.'

"For many are called, but few are chosen."

Religious Leaders Ask Jesus about Paying Taxes

Then went the Pharisees, and took counsel how they might entangle him in his words, so that they might deliver him unto the power and authority of the governor.

And they watched him, and sent out unto him their disciples with the Herodians, saying, Master we know that thou art true, and teachest the way of God in truth, neither regardest not the person of any men.

What thinkest thou? Is it lawful to give tribute unto Caesar, or not? But knowing their hypocrisy, Jesus perceived their craftiness, and wickedness and said, **Why tempt ye me, ye hypocrite? Show me the tribute,** and they brought unto him a penny. And he saith unto them, **Whose is this image and superscription**? They saith unto him, Caesar's. And Jesus answering said unto them, **Render to Caesar the things that are Caesar's and to God the things that are God's.** When they had heard these words, they marveled at his answer, and could not take hold of his words before the people: and held their peace, and left him, and went their way.

QUESTIONS ABOUT RESURRECTION

The same day came to him certain of the Sadducees, which deny that there is any resurrection; and they asked him, saying, Master, Moses wrote unto us, If any man's brother die, leaving his wife behind him, without children, that his brother should take his wife, marry her, and raise up children unto his brother. Now there were seven brethren: and the first, when he had married a wife, deceased, having no children. And the second took her to wife, and he died childless. And the third took her; and in like manner the seven also: and they left no children, and died. Last of all the woman died also. Therefore in the resurrection, when they shall rise, whose wife shall she be of them? for the seven had her to wife.

Jesus said unto to them, **do ye not therefore err, Because ye know not the scriptures, neither the power of God? The children of this world marry, and are given in marriage: But they which shall be accounted worthy to obtain the world, and the resurrection from the dead, either marry, nor are given in marriage: Neither can they die any more: for they are equal unto the angels; and are the children of God, and of the resurrection. Now that the dead are raised, even Moses showed at the bush, when he calleth the Lord the God of Abraham, and the God of Isaac, and the God of Jacob. For he is not a God of the dead, but of the living: for all live unto him.**

Then certain of the scribes answering said, Master, thou hast well said. And after that they durst not ask him any question at all. And when the multitude heard this, they were astonished at his doctrine.

Religious Leaders Question Jesus about the Greatest Commandment

But when the scribes and Pharisees gathered and heard that he had put the Sadducees to silence, they reasoned together. Then one of them, which was a lawyer, asked him a question, tempting him, saying, Master, which is the greatest commandment in the law? Jesus, said unto him, **Thou shalt love the Lord thy God with all thy heart, and with all thy soul, and with all thy mind. This is the first and greatest commandment. And the second is like unto it, Thou shalt love thy neighbor as thyself. On these two commandments hang all the law and the prophets. There is none other commandment greater than these.**

And the scribe said unto him, Well, Master, thou hast sayest the truth: for there is but one God; and there is none other but He: and to love him with all thy heart, and with all thine understanding, and with all thy soul, and with all thine strength, and to love his neighbor as himself, is more than all whole burnt offerings and sacrifices. And when Jesus saw that he answered discreetly, he said unto him, **Thou art not far from the kingdom of God.**

LEADERS CANNOT ANSWER JESUS

While Jesus taught in the temple, and the Pharisees were gathered together, And Jesus asked them, saying, **The scribes say that Christ is the Son of David? What think ye of Christ Whose son is he?** They said unto him, the son of David. **How then doth David himself, in the book of Psalms by the Holy Ghost, say, The Lord said unto my Lord, Sit thou on my right hand, till I make thine enemies thy footstool? Therefore if David then call him Lord, how is he his son?** And no man was able to answer him a word, neither durst any man from day forth ask him any more questions. But the common people heard him gladly.

Warning against Religious Leaders

Then in the audience of all the people, spake Jesus to his disciples, saying, **The scribes and the Pharisees sit in Moses' seat: All therefore whatsoever they bid you observe, that and do: But do not ye after their works: for they say, and do not. But beware of them because they love to go in long clothing, and love salutations in the marketplaces, and the chief seats in the synagogues, and uppermost rooms at the feasts: Which devour widows' houses, and for a pretence make long prayers: these shall receive greater damnation.**

For they bind heavy burdens that are laid upon men's shoulders grievous to be borne, but they themselves will not move them with one of their fingers. But all their works they do for to be seen of men: they make broad their phylacteries, and enlarge the borders of their garments, and love to be called of men, Rabbi, But be not ye called Rabbi: for one is your Master, even Christ and all ye are brethren. And call no man your father upon the earth: for one is your Father, which is in heaven. Neither be ye called masters: for one is your Master, even Christ. But he that is greatest among you shall be your servant. And whosoever shall exalt himself shall be abased; and he that shall humble himself shall be exalted.

JESUS CONDEMNS RELIGIOUS LEADERS

But woe unto you, scribes and Pharisees, hypocrites! for ye shut up the kingdom of heaven against men: for ye neither go in yourselves, neither suffer ye them that are entering to go in. Woe unto you, scribes and Pharisees, hypocrites! for ye devour widows' houses, and for a pretence make long prayer: therefore ye shall receive the greater damnation. Woe unto you, scribes and Pharisees, hypocrites! for ye compass sea and land to make one proselyte, and when he is made, ye make him twofold more the child of hell than yourselves. Woe unto you, ye blind guides, which say, whosoever shall swear by the temple, it is nothing; but whosoever shall swear by the gold of the temple, he is a debtor! Ye fools and blind: for whether is greater, the gold, or the temple that sanctifieth the gold? And, whosoever shall swear by the altar, it is nothing; but whosoever sweareth by the gift that is upon it, he is guilty. Ye fools and blind: for whether is greater, the gift, or the altar that sanctifieth the gift? Whoso therefore shall swear by the altar, sweareth by it, and by all things thereon. And whoso shall swear by the temple, sweareth by it, and by him that dwelleth therein. And he that shall swear by heaven, sweareth by the throne of God, and by him that sitteth thereon.

Woe unto you, scribes and Pharisees, hypocrites! for ye pay tithe of mint and anise and cummin, and have omitted the weightier matters of the law, judgment, mercy, and faith: these ought ye to have done, and not to leave the other undone. Ye blind guides, which strain at a gnat, and swallow a camel. Woe unto you, scribes and Pharisees, hypocrites! for ye make clean the outside of the cup and of the platter, but within they are full of extortion and excess. Thou blind Pharisee, cleanse first that which is within the cup and platter, that the outside of them may be clean also.

Woe unto you, scribes and Pharisees, hypocrites! for ye are like unto whited sepulchres, which indeed appear beautiful outward, but are within full of dead men's bones, and of all uncleanness. Even so ye also outwardly appear righteous unto men, but within ye are full of hypocrisy and iniquity. Woe unto you, scribes and Pharisees, hypocrites! because ye build the tombs of the prophets, and garnish the sepulchres of the righteous, and say, If we had been in the days of our fathers, we would not have been partakers with them in the blood of the prophets.

Wherefore ye be witnesses unto yourselves, that ye are the children of them which killed the prophets. Fill ye up then the measure of your fathers. Ye serpents, ye generation of vipers, how can ye escape the damnation of hell?

Wherefore, behold, I send unto you prophets, and wise men, and scribes: and some of them ye shall kill and crucify; and some of them shall ye scourge in your synagogues, and persecute them from city to city: That upon you may come all the righteous blood shed upon the earth, from the blood of righteous Abel unto the blood of Zacharias son of Barachias, whom ye slew between the temple and the altar. Verily I say unto you, All these things shall come upon this generation.

Jesus Grieves Over Jerusalem Again

O Jerusalem, Jerusalem, thou that killest the prophets, and stonest them which are sent unto thee, how often would I have gathered thy chicks together, even as a hen gathereth her chickens under her wings, and ye would not! Behold, your house is left unto you desolate. For I say unto you, Ye shall not see me henceforth, till ye shall say, Blessed is he that cometh in the name of the Lord.

WIDOW GIVES ALL SHE HAS

And Jesus sat over against the treasury, looked up and beheld how the people cast money into the treasury: and many that were rich cast in much.

And there came a certain poor widow, and she threw in two mites, which make a farthing. And he called unto him his disciples, and saith unto them, **Verily I say unto you, That this poor widow hath cast more in, than all they which have cast into the treasury: For all they did cast in of their abundance; but she of her want did cast in all that she had, even all her living.**

JESUS TELLS ABOUT THE FUTURE

And as Jesus went out of the temple: with his disciples, and rumors arose about him, some came to him and spake, Master see what manner of buildings, and the temple, adorned with goodly stones and gifts. Then answered Jesus and said unto them, **Seeth thou these great building? Behold the days will come, in the which there shall not be left one stone upon another, that shall not be thrown down.** And as he sat upon the mount of Olives over against the temple, the disciples Peter, James, John, and Andrew came unto him privately, saying, Master, when shall these things be? And what shall be the sign of thy coming, and what shall be the sign when all these things shall be fulfilled? And the end of the world?

Take heed lest any man deceive you: The time draweth near: For many shall come in my name, saying, I am Christ; and shall deceive many, go ye not therefore after them. And ye shall hear of wars and rumours of wars: and commotions, for nation shall rise against nation, and kingdom against kingdom: and there shall be earthquakes in divers places, and great fearful sights and great signs shall there be from heaven. There shall be famines and troubles: see that ye be not troubled: for all these things must come to pass, but the end is not yet. All these are the beginning of sorrows.

But before all these, they shall lay their hands upon you, and persecute you, delivering ye up to the synagogues, and into prisons, being brought before kings and rulers for my name's sake. And it shall turn unto you for a testimony.

They will deliver ye up to be afflicted, and some will try to kill you: And then shall many be offended, and shall betray one another, and shall hate one another: And many false prophets shall rise and shall deceive many. And because iniquity shall abound the love of most shall wax cold, and ye shall be hated of all nations for my name's sake. Settle it therefore in your hearts, not to meditate before what ye shall answer: For I will give you a mouth and wisdom, through the Holy Spirit to speak, which all your adversaries shall not be able to gainsay nor resist.

Andyeshallbebetrayedbothbyparents,andbrethren, kinsfolks, and friends; and some of you shall they cause to be put to death. And ye shall be hated of all men for my name's sake. But there shall not a hair of your head perish. To he who shall endure unto the end, in your patience possess ye your souls. And this gospel of the kingdom shall be preached in all the world for a witness unto all nations; and then shall the end come. And when ye shall see Jerusalem compassed with armies, knowththatthedesolationthereofisnigh. AndWhenyou therefore shall see the abomination of desolation, spoken of by Daniel the prophet, stand in the holy place, (whoso readeth, let him understand:)

And let them which be in Judaea flee into the mountains: Let them which is on the housetop not come to take anything out of his house: Neither let him which is in the field return back to take his clothes. And woe unto them that are with child, and unto them that give suck in those days! But pray that your flight be not in the winter neither on the sabbath day: For then shall be great tribulation, distress in the land, and wrath upon this people, they shall fall by the edge of the sword, and shall be led away captive into all nations: and Jerusalem shall be trodden down of the Gentiles, until the times of the Gentiles be fulfilled such as was not since the beginning of the world, unto this time, no, nor ever shall be. And except those days should be shortened, there should no flesh be saved: but for the elects sake those days shall be shortened. Then if any man shall say unto you, Lo, here is Christ, or there; believe it not. For there shall arise false Christ and false prophets, showing, great signs and wonders; insomuch that, if it were possible, that they shall deceive the very elect. Behold, I have told you before.

Jesus Tells about His Return

But in those days, after that tribulation, and there shall be signs in the sun, and in the moon, and in the stars; and upon the earth distress of nations, with perplexity; the sea and the waves roaring; For as the lightning cometh out of the east, and shineth even unto the west; so shall also the coming of the Son of man be. For wheresoever the carcase is, there will the eagles be gathered together. Men's hearts will failth them for fear, and for looking after those things which are coming upon the earth.

Immediately after the tribulation of those days shall the sun be darkened, the moon shall not give her light, and the stars shall fall from the heavens, and the powers of the heavens shall be shaken: And then shall appear the sign of the Son of man in air. Then shall all the tribes of the earth mourn, and they shall see the Son of man coming in the clouds of heaven with power and great glory. And he shall send his angels with a great sound of a trumpet, and they shall gather together his elect from the four winds, from one end of heavens to the other.

Now learn a parable of the fig tree; When her branch is yet tender, and putteth forth leaves, ye know that summer is near: So ye in like manner, when ye shall see these things come to pass, know ye that the kingdom of God is nigh at hand, even at the door. Verily I say unto you, that this generation shall not pass, till all these things be done. Heaven and earth shall pass away: but my words shall not pass away.

Jesus Tells about Being Watchful

Take heed to yourselves, lest at any time your hearts be overcharged with surfeiting, and drunkenness, and the cares of this life, so that day come not upon you unawares. For as a snare shall come on all them that are on the face of the whole earth. Watch ye therefore, and pray always, that ye may be accounted worthy to escape all these things that shall come to pass, and to stand before the Son of man. For the Son of man is as a man taking a far journey, who left his house, and gave authority to his servants, and every man his work, and commanded the porter to watch. Watch ye therefore: for ye know not what hour the master of the house cometh, at even, or at midnight, or at the cockcrowing, or in the morning: Lest coming suddenly he find you sleeping. For what I say unto you I say unto all, Watch!

But of that day and hour knoweth no man, no, not the angels of heaven, neither the Son, but the Father. For as in the days of Noah just before the flood, so shall also the coming of the Son of man be. For they were eating and drinking, marrying and being giving in marriage, until the day that Noah entered into the ark, and knew not until the flood came, and took them all away; so shall also the coming of the Son of man be. There shall be two in the field; the one shall be taken, and the other left. Two women shall be grinding at the mill; the one shall be taken, and the other left. Watch therefore: for ye know not what hour your Lord doth come.

But know this, that if the goodman of the house had known in what hour the thief would come, he would have watched, and would not have suffered his house to be broken up. Therefore be ye ready: for in such an hour as ye think not the Son of man cometh.

Who then is a faithful and wise servant, whom his lord hath made ruler over his household, to give them meat in due season? Blessed is that servant, whom his lord when he cometh shall find him so doing. Verily I say unto you, that he shall make him ruler over all his goods. But and if that evil servant shall say in his

heart, My lord delayeth his coming; And shall begin to smite his fellowservants, and to eat and drink with the drunken; The lord of that servant shall come in a day when he looketh not for him, and in an hour that he is not aware of, And shall cut him asunder, and appoint him his portion with the hypocrites: there shall be weeping and gnashing of teeth.

Jesus Tells about Parable Of Ten Bridesmaids

Then the kingdom of heaven shall be likened to ten virgins who took their lamps and went out to meet the bridegroom. Now five of them were wise, and five were foolish. Those who were foolish took their lamps and took no oil with them, but the wise took oil in their vessels with their lamps. But while the bridegroom was delayed, they all slumbered and slept. "And at midnight a cry was heard: 'Behold, the bridegroom is coming; go out to meet him!' Then all those virgins arose and trimmed their lamps. And the foolish said to the wise, 'Give us some of your oil, for our lamps are going out.' But the wise answered, saying, 'No, lest there should not be enough for us and you; but go ye rather unto those who sell, and buy for yourselves.' And while they went to buy, the bridegroom came, and those who were ready went in with him unto the wedding; and the door was shut. "Afterward the other virgins came also, saying, 'Lord, Lord, open unto us!' But he answered and saith, 'Assuredly, I say to you, I know ye not.

"Watch therefore, for you know neither the day nor the hour in which the Son of Man is coming.

Jesus Tells the Parable Of the Loaned Money

"For the kingdom of heaven is like a man traveling to a far country, whom called his own servants and delivered his goods unto them. And to one he gave five talents, unto another two, and to another one, unto each according to his own ability; and immediately he went on a journey. Then he who had received the five talents went and traded with them, and made another five talents. And likewise he who had received two gained two more also. But he who had received one went and dug in the ground, and hid his lord's money. After a long time the lord of those servants came and settled accounts with them. "So he who had received five talents came and brought five other talents, saying, 'Lord, you delivered unto me five talents; look, I have gained five more talents besides them.' His lord said unto him, 'Well done, good and faithful servant; you were faithful over a few things,

I will make you ruler over many things. Enter into the joy of your lord.' He also who had received two talents came and saith, 'Lord, ye delivered unto me two talents; look, I have gained two more talents besides them.' His lord said unto him, 'Well done, good and faithful servant; ye have been faithful over a few things, I will make you ruler over many things. Enter into the joy of your lord.' "Then he who had received the one talent came and saith, 'Lord, I knew you to be a hard man, reaping where you have not sown, and gathering where ye have not scattered seed. And I was afraid, and went and hid your talent in the ground. Look, there ye have what is yours.' "But his lord answered and said unto him, 'You wicked and lazy servant, ye knew that I reap where I have not sown, and gather where I have not scattered seed. So you ought to have deposited my money with the bankers, and at my coming I would have received back my own with interest. So take the talent from him, and give it unto him who has ten talents.

'For to everyone who has, more will be given, and he will have abundance; but from him who does not have, even what he has

will be taken away. And cast the unprofitable servant into the outer darkness. There will be weeping and gnashing of teeth.

Jesus Tells of the Final Judgment

"When the Son of Man comes in His glory, and all the holy angels with Him, He will sit upon the throne of His glory. All the nations will be gathered before Him, and He will separate them one from another, as a shepherd divides his sheep from the goats. And He will set the sheep upon His right hand, but the goats on the left. Then the King will say unto those on His right hand, 'Come, you blessed of My Father, inherit the kingdom prepared for you from the foundation of the world: for I was hungry and ye gave Me food; I was thirsty and ye gave Me drink; I was a stranger and ye took Me in; I was naked and ye clothed Me; I was sick and ye visited Me; I was in prison and ye came unto Me.' "Then the righteous will answer Him, saying, 'Lord, when did we see You hungry and feed you, or thirsty and give Ye drink? When did we see Ye a stranger and take You in, or naked and clothe You? Or when did we see Ye sick, or in prison, and come unto You?' And the King will answer and say unto them, 'Assuredly, I say to you, inasmuch as ye did it to one of the least of these My brethren, ye did it unto Me.'

"Then He will also say unto those on the left hand, 'Depart from Me, ye cursed, into the everlasting fire prepared for the devil and his angels: for I was hungry and ye gave Me no food; I was thirsty and ye gave Me no drink; I was a stranger and you did not take Me in, naked and ye did not clothe Me, sick and in prison and you did not visit Me.'

"Then they also will answer Him, saying, 'Lord, when did we see You hungry or thirsty or a stranger or naked or sick or in prison, and did not minister unto You?' Then He will answer them, saying, 'Assuredly, I say unto you, inasmuch as ye did not do it to one of the least of these, you did not do it unto Me. and these will go away into everlasting punishment, but the righteous into eternal life."

The Conspiracy against Jesus

And it came to pass, when Jesus finished all these saying, He said unto his disciples, **Ye know the time draweth near. In two days is the Passover the feast of unleavened beard and the Son of man is to be betrayed and crucified.**

Then assembled together the chief priests, the scribes, and the elders of the people, unto the palace of the high priest, who was called Caiaphas, and consulted how they might take Jesus by subtilty, but not on the feast day, so as not to cause and uproar, for they feared the people.

What then do we? For this man doeth many miracles. If we let him thus alone, all men will believe on him: and the Romans shall come and take away both our place and nation.

Then Caiaphas, being the high priest that same year, said unto them, Ye know nothing at all, nor consider, that it is expedient for us, that one man should die for the nation then that the whole nation perish not. And this spake he not of himself, but being high priest, he prophesied that Jesus should die. And not for that nation abroad only, but for the whole would. From that day forth they sought together, how they might put him to death.

Judas Agrees to Betray Jesus

Then Satan entered into Judas surnamed Iscariot, being of the number of the twelve, and went his way to commune with chief priests and captains, how he might betray him unto them, what will ye giveth me if I deliver Him unto You, And when they heard it, they were glad, and covenanted, with him for thirty pieces of silver. Then he promised from that time forth that he would sought opportunity to betray him unto them in the absence of the multitude.

Preparation for the Passover

Now it was the first day of the feast of unleavened bread, when the passover lamb was to be killed, his disciples came unto him saying to him, Where wilt thou that we go and prepare that thou mayest eat the passover?

And he sendeth forth two of His disciples, John and Peter, and saith unto them, **Go ye into the city, and there shall meet you a man bearing a pitcher of water: Follow him into wheresoever house he entereth, and say ye to the goodman of the house, The Master saith, My time is at hand, Where is the guest chamber, where I shall eat the passover with my disciples? He will show you large upper room, furnished and prepare.** And his disciples went forth as Jesus comanded them, and came into the city, and found just as he had said unto them: and they made ready the passover.

The Last Supper

And as the hour had come, in the evening, He sat down, with the twelve apostles. And he said unto them, **With desire I have desired to eat this passover with you before I suffer: For I say unto you, I will not any more eat thereof, until it be fulfilled in the kingdom of God.**

And as they did eat, He took bread, blessed it, and broke it, and gave it unto the disciples, and said, **Take, eat; this is my body, which is given for you: this do in remembrance of me. And then he took the cup, and when He had given thanks, gave it to them, saying, Drink ye all of it; For this is my blood, the blood of the new testament, which is shed for you, and many for the remission of sins. But I say unto you, I will drink no more of the fruit of the vine, until that day that I drink it new in the kingdom of God.**

The One Which Betrayeth "Jesus"

But, behold, I tell ye that one of you which eateth with me. By his hand shall it be of him that betrayeth me. Indeed, truly the Son of man goeth, as it was determined: and written of him, but woe unto that man by whom he is betrayed! For it would be better if that man had never been born. And they all became exceeding sorrowful. Then the disciples looked everyone, at one another, doubting of whom he spake, who should do this thing, and began to say unto him, Lord, is it I? And another said, Is it I? Then Judas, which betrayed him, answered and said, Master, is it I? Jesus said, **Thou hast said.**

Now there was leaning on Jesus bosom one of his disciples, whom he loved. Then Simon Peter therefore beckoned unto him, that he should ask of him of whom he spake. Jesus answered, **He it is, to whom I shall give a sop, when I have dipped it.** And when he had dipped the sop, he gave it unto Judas Iscariot, the son of Simon. And after he had received it, Satan entered into him. Then said Jesus unto him, **What thou doest, do quickly.** Now no man at the table knew for what intent Jesus had said this unto him; But thought he might go to buy those things that we have need of against the feast; or, that he should give something to the poor. He then having received the sop went immediately out: and it was night.

I Am the Way, the Truth, and the Life:

Then said Jesus unto them: **Let not your heart be troubled: ye believe in God, believe also in me. In my Father's house are many mansions: if it were not so, I would have told You.**

And if I go and prepare a place for you, I will come again, and receive you unto myself; that where I am, there ye may be also. And whither I go ye know, and the way ye know.

Thomas saith unto him, Lord, we know not whither thou goest; and how can we know the way?

Jesus saith unto him, **I am the way, the truth, and the life: no man cometh unto the Father, but by me. If ye had known me, ye should have known my Father also: and from henceforth ye know him, and have seen him.** Philip saith unto him, Lord, show us the Father, and it will be sufficeth for us. Jesus saith unto him, **Have I been so long a time with you, and yet hast thou not known me, Philip? He that hath seen me hath seen the Father; and how sayest thou then, show us the Father? Believest thou not that I am in the Father, and the Father in me? The words that I speak unto you I speak not of myself: but the Father that dwelleth in me, he doeth the works. Believe me that I am in the Father, and the Father in me: or else believe me for the very works' sake. Verily, verily, I say unto you, He that believeth on me, the works that I do shall he do also; and greater works than these shall he do; because I go unto my Father.**

And whatsoever ye shall ask in my name, that will I do, that the Father may be glorified in the Son. If ye shall ask any thing in my name, I will do it.

Jesus Washes the Feet of His Disciples

Jesus knew that his hour was come that he should depart out of this world unto the Father, having loved his own which were in the world, unto the end. And supper being ended, and Satan having now put into the heart of Judas Iscariot, Simon's *son*, to betray him; Jesus knowing that the Father had given all things into his hands, and that he was come from God, and went to God;

He riseth, and laid aside his garments; and took a towel, and girded himself. After that he poureth water into a basin, and began to wash the disciples' feet, and to wipe them with the towel wherewith he was girded. Then cometh he unto Simon Peter: and Peter saith to him, Lord, dost thou wash my feet? Jesus answered and said unto him, **What I do thou knowest not now; but thou shalt know hereafter.** Peter saith unto him, Thou shalt never wash my feet. **Jesus answered him, If I wash thee not, thou hast no part with me.** Simon Peter saith unto him, Lord, not my feet only, but also my hands and my head.

Jesus saith unto him, **He that is washed needeth not save to wash his feet, but is clean every whit: and ye are clean, but not all.** For he knew who should betray him; therefore said he, **Ye are not all clean.** So after he had washed their feet, and had taken his garments, and was set down again, he said unto them, **Know ye what I have done to you? Ye call me Master and Lord: and ye say well; for so I am. If I then, your Lord and Master, have washed your feet; ye also ought to wash one another's feet. For I have given you an example, that ye should do as I have done to you. Verily, verily, I say unto you, The** servant is not greater than his lord; neither he that is sent greater than he that sent him. If ye know these things, happy are ye if ye do them. I speak not of you all: I know whom I have chosen: but that the scripture may be fulfilled, He that eateth bread with me hath lifted up his heel against me. Now I tell you before it comth, that, when it is come to pass, ye may believe that I am he. Verily, verily, I say unto you, He that receiveth whomsoever I send receiveth me; and he that receiveth me receiveth him that sent me.

Which One of Us Be Accounted the Greatest

And there was also a strife among them, which of them should be accounted the greatest. And he said unto them, **The kings of the Gentiles exercise lordship over them; and they exercise authority upon them are called benefactors. But ye shall not be so: but he is greatest among you, let him be as the younger; and he that is chief, as he that doth serve. For whether is greater, he that setteth at meat, or he that serveth? Is not he that setteth at meat? But I am among you as he that serveth. Ye are they which have continued with me in my temptations. And I appoint unto you a kingdom, as my Father hath appointed unto me; that ye may eat and drink at my table in my kingdom, and sit on thrones judging the twelve tribes of Israel.**

Jesus Predicts Peter's Denial

Then said Jesus; **Now is the Son of man glorified, and God is glorified in him. If God be glorified in him, God shall also glorify him in himself, and shall straightway glorify him. Little children, yet a little while I am with you. Ye shall seek me: and as I said unto the Jews, Whither I go, ye cannot come; so now I say to you. A new commandment I give unto you, that ye love one another; as I have loved you, that ye also love one another. By this shall all men know that ye are my disciples, if ye have love one another.** Simon Peter said unto him, Lord, whither goest thou? Jesus answered him **Whither I go, thou canst not follow me now; but thou shalt follow me afterwards.** Peter said unto him, Lord, why cannot I follow thee now? I will lay down my life for thy sake. Jesus answered him, **Wilt thou lay down thy life for my sake? For I say unto you, Peter the cock shall not crow this day, before thou hath thrice deny that thou knowest me.**

And the Lord said, **Simon, Simon, behold, Satan hath desired to have you, that he may sift you as wheat: But I have prayed for thee, that thy faith fail not: and when thou art converted, strengthen thy brethren.** And he said unto them, **When I sent you without purse, and scrip, and shoes, lacked ye any thing? And they said, Nothing. Then said he unto them, But now, he that hath a purse, let him take it, and likewise his scrip: and he that hath no sword, let him sell his garment, and buy one. For I say unto you, that this that is written must yet be accomplished in me, and he was reckoned**

among the transgressors: for the things concerning me have an end. And they said, Lord, behold, here are two swords. And he said unto them, **It is enough.**

Jesus Promises the Holy Spirit

"If you love Me, keepth My commandments. And I will pray unto the Father, and He will give ye another Helper, that he may abide with you forever. Even the Spirit of truth, whom the world cannot receive, because it neither sees Him nor knows Him; but ye know Him, for He dwells with you and will be in you. I will not leave ye orphans; I will come unto you.

"A little while longer and the world will see me no more, but ye shall see me. Because I live, you will live also. At that day ye will know that I am in My Father, and ye in me, and I in you. He who has my commandments and keepth them, it is he who loves Me. And he who loves me will be loved by My Father, and I will love him and manifest Myself unto him." Judas (not Iscariot) said unto Him, "Lord, how is it that You will manifest Yourself unto us, and not unto the world?" Jesus answered and saith to him, **"If anyone loves Me, he will keep My word; and My Father will love him, and We will come unto him and make Our home within him. He who does not love Me does not keep My words; and the word which ye hear is not Mine but the Father's who sent Me.**

"These things I have spoken unto you while being present with you. But the Helper, the Holy Spirit, whom the Father will send in My name, He will teach ye all things, and bring to your remembrance all things that I said unto you. Peace I leave with you, My peace I give unto you; not as the world gives do I give to ye. Let not your heart be not troubled, neither let it be afraid. Ye have heard Me say unto you, 'I am going away and coming back unto you.' If you loved Me, ye would rejoice because I said, 'I am going to the Father; for my Father is greater than I. And now I have told you before it comes, that when it does come to pass, ye may believe. I will no longer talk much with you, for the ruler of this world is coming, and he has nothing in Me. But that the world may know that I love the Father, and as the Father gave Me commandment, so I do.

Jesus Teaches about the Vine and the Branches

I am the true vine, and my Father is the husbandman. Every branch in me that beareth not fruit he taketh away: and every branch that beareth fruit, he purgeth it, that it may bring forth more fruit. Now ye are clean through the word which I have spoken unto you. Abide in me, and I in you. As the branch cannot bear fruit of itself, except it abide in the vine; no more can ye, except ye abide in me. I am the vine, ye are the branches: He that abideth in me, and I in him, the same bringeth forth much fruit: for without me ye can do nothing. If a man abide not in me, he is cast forth as a branch, and is withered; and men gather them, and cast them into the fire, and they are burned. If ye abide in me, and my words abide in you, ye shall ask what ye will, and it shall be done unto you.

Herein is my Father glorified, that ye bear much fruit; so shall ye be my disciples. As the Father hath loved me, so have I loved you: continue ye in my love. If ye keep my commandments, ye shall abide in my love; even as I have kept my Father's commandments, and abide in his love. These things have I spoken unto you, that my joy might remain in you, and that your joy might be full. This is my commandment, That ye love one another, as I have loved you. Greater love hath no man than this, that a man lay down his life for his friends. Ye are my friends, if ye do whatsoever I command you. Henceforth I call you not servants; for the servant knoweth not what his lord doeth: but I have called you friends; for all things that I have heard of my Father I have made known unto you. Ye have not chosen me, but I have chosen you, and ordained you, that ye should go and bring forth fruit, and that your fruit should remain: that whatsoever ye shall ask of the Father in my name, he may give it you.

Jesus Warns about the World's Hatred

If the world hates you, ye know that it hated me before it hated you. If ye were of the world, the world would love his own: but because ye are not of the world, but I have chosen you out of the world, therefore the world hateth you. Remember the word that I said unto you, The servant is not greater than his lord. If they have persecuted me, they will also persecute you; if they have kept my saying, they will keep yours also. But all these things will they do unto you for my name's sake, because they know not him that sent me. If I had not come and spoken unto them, they had not had sin: but now they have no cloak for their sin. He that hateth me hateth my Father also. If I had not done among them the works which none other man did, they had not had sin: but now have they both seen and hated both me and my Father. But this cometh to pass, that the word might be fulfilled that is written in their law, They hated me without a cause. But when the Comforter is come, whom I will send unto you from the Father, even the Spirit of truth, which proceedeth from the Father, he shall testify of me: But these things have I told you, that when the time shall come, ye may remember that I told you of them. And these things I said not unto you at the beginning, because I was with you.

Jesus Teaches about the Holy Spirit

But now I go my way unto him that sent me; and none of you asketh me, Whither goest thou? But because I have said these things unto you, sorrow hath filled your heart. Nevertheless I tell you the truth; It is expedient for you that I go away: for if I go not away, the Comforter will not come unto you; but if I depart, I will send him unto you. And when he is come, he will reprove the world of sin, and of righteousness, and of judgment: because they believe not on me; Of righteousness, because I go unto my Father, and ye see me no more; Of judgment, because the prince of this world is judged. I have yet many things to say unto you, but ye cannot bear them now. Howbeit when he, the Spirit of truth, is comth, he will guide you into all truth: for he shall not speak of himself; but whatsoever he shall hear, that shall he speak: and he will show you things that comth. He shall glorify me: for he shall receive of mine, and shall show it unto you. All things that the Father hath are mine: therefore said I, that he shall take of mine, and shall show it unto you. A little while, and ye shall not see me: and again, a little while, and ye shall see me, because I go to the Father.

Jesus Teaches about Using His Name in Prayer

Then said some of his disciples among themselves, What is this that he saith unto us, A little while, and ye shall not see me: and again, a little while, and ye shall see me: and, Because I go to the Father? They said therefore, What is this that he saith, A little while? we cannot tell what he saith. Now Jesus knew that they were desirous to ask him, and said unto them, **Do ye inquire among yourselves of that I said, A little while, and ye shall not see me: and again, a little while, and ye shall see me? Verily, verily, I say unto you, That ye shall weep and lament, but the world shall rejoice: and ye shall be sorrowful, but your sorrow shall be turned into joy. A woman when she is in travail hath sorrow, because her hour is come: but as soon as she is delivered of the child, she remembereth no more the anguish, for joy that a man is born into the world. And ye now therefore have sorrow: but I will see you again, and your heart shall rejoice, and your joy no man taketh from you. And in that day ye shall ask me nothing. Verily, verily, I say unto you, Whatsoever ye shall ask the Father in my name, he will give it you.**

Hitherto have ye asked nothing in my name: ask, and ye shall receive, that your joy may be full. These things have I spoken unto you in proverbs: but the time cometh, when I shall no more speak unto you in proverbs, but I shall show you plainly of the Father. At that day ye shall ask in my name: and I say not unto you, that I will pray the Father for you: For the Father himself loveth you, because ye have loved me, and have believed that I came out from

God. I came forth from the Father, and am come into the world: again, I leave the world, and go to the Father. His disciples said unto him, Lo, now speakest thou plainly, and speakest no proverb. Now are we sure that thou knowest all things, and needest not that any man should ask thee: by this we believe that thou camest forth from God. Jesus answered them, **Do ye now believe? Behold, the hour cometh, yea, is now come, that ye shall be scattered, every man to his own, and shall leave me alone: and yet I am not alone, because the Father is with me. These things I have spoken unto you, that in me ye might have peace. In the world ye shall have tribulation: but be of good cheer; I have overcome the world.**

Jesus Prays for Himself

These words spake Jesus, and lifted up his eyes unto heaven, and said, **Father, the hour is come; glorify thy Son, that thy Son also may glorify thee: As thou hast given him power over all flesh, that he should give eternal life to as many as thou hast given him. And this is life eternal, that they might know thee the only true God, and Jesus Christ, whom thou hast sent. I have glorified thee on the earth: I have finished the work which thou gavest me to do. And now, O Father, glorify thou me with thine own self with the glory which I had with thee before the world was.**

He Prays for His Disciples

I have manifested thy name unto the men which thou gavest me out of the world: thine they were, and thou gavest them unto me; and they have kept thy word. Now they have known that all things whatsoever thou hast given me are of thee. For I have given unto them the words which thou gavest me; and they have received them, and have known surely that I came out from thee, and they have believed that thou didst send me. I pray for them: I pray not for the world, but for them which thou hast given me; for they are thine. And all mine are thine, and thine are mine; and I am glorified in them.

And now I am no more in the world, but these are in the world, and I come to thee. Holy Father, keep through thine own name those whom thou hast given me, that they may be one, as we are. While I was with them in the world, I kept them in thy name: those that thou gavest me I have kept, and none of them is lost, but the son of perdition; that the scripture might be fulfilled. And now come I unto thee; and these things I speak in the world, that they might have my joy fulfilled in themselves.

I have given them thy word; and the world hath hated them, because they are not of the world, even as I am not of the world. I pray not that thou should take them out of the world, but that thou should keep them from the evil. They are not of the world, even as I am not of the world. Sanctify them through thy truth: thy word is truth. As thou hast sent me into the world, even so have I also sent them into the world. And for their sakes I sanctify myself, that they also might be sanctified through the truth.

Jesus Prays For Future Believers

Neither pray I for these alone, but for them also which shall believe on me through their word; That they all may be one; as thou, Father, art in me, and I in thee, that they also may be one in us: that the world may believe that thou hast sent me. And the glory which thou gavest me I have given them; that they may be one, even as we are one: I in them, and thou in me, that they may be made perfect in one; and that the world may know that thou hast sent me, and hast loved them, as thou hast loved me.

Father, I will that they also, whom thou hast given me, be with me where I am; that they may behold my glory, which thou hast given me: for thou lovedst me before the foundation of the world. O righteous Father, the world hath not known thee: but I have known thee, and these have known that thou hast sent me. And I have declared unto them thy name, and will declare it: that the love wherewith thou hast loved me may be in them, and I in them.

Jesus Again Predicts Peter's Denial

(And when they had sung a hymn, they went out into
the mount of Olives.)
Then saith Jesus unto them, **All ye shall be offended because of me
this night: for it is written, I will smite the shepherd, and the sheep
of the flock shall be scattered abroad.**

But after I am rise again, I will go before you into Galilee. But
Peter answered and said unto him, Though all men shall be offended
because of thee, yet will I never be offended. Jesus said unto him,
**Verily I say unto thee, That this day, even in this night, before the
cock crow twice, thou shalt deny me thrice. But again Peter said
unto him, and spake the more vehemently, If I should die with
thee, I will not deny thee in any wise. Likewise also said they all.**

Jesus Agonizes in the Garden

And he came out, with his disciples, over the kendorn brook coming unto a place called Gethsemane, also called the Mount of Olives; saying unto them, **Sit ye here, while I go and pray yonder.** And he took with him Peter and the two sons of Zebedee, James and John, and began to be very heavy and sorrowful. **Then saith he unto them, My soul is exceeding sorrowful, even unto death: Pray that ye enter not into temptation. Tarry here with me and watch.** And he withdrawn from them about a stones cast, fell to the ground, kneeling, with his face down, Saying, **Aba, O my Father, if thou be willing, let this hour pass from me, for all things are possible unto thee, take away this cup from me: nevertheless not what I will, but thine, wilt, be done.**

And when he came back unto his disciples, He findeth them asleep, and said unto **Simon Peter, sleepiest thou? couldest not thou watch one hour, pray, lest ye enter not into temptation: the spirit indeed is willing, but the flesh is weak.** He again went away the second time, and prayed, saying **"O" my Father; if this cup may not pass away from me, except I drink of it, (nevertheless thy will be done).**

And he came and found them asleep again: for their eyes were heavy, and he left them, and went way again, and prayed the third time, saying the same words.

And being in agony he prayed more earnestly: and his sweat was as it were great drops of blood falling upon the ground. *An angel appeared to strengthen him.* And when He was flinched, He rose up from prayer, and cometh, again to his disciples, and said unto them, **Sleep on now, and take your rest:**

(It is enough), rise the hour is come; behold, Son of man is betrayed into the hands of sinners. Rise, let us go; (lo, he that betrayeth me is at hand).

Jesus Is Betrayed And Arrested

And while he yet spake, lo, Judas came having received a band of men, from the chief priests, with officers and Pharisees, elders of the people and a great multitude with swords and staves. Jesus therefore, knowing all things that should come upon him, went forth, and said unto them, **Whom seek ye?** They answered him, Jesus of Nazareth. Jesus saith unto them,

I am "He"

As soon they heard him say I am He, they withdrew back, and fell to the ground. Then asked he them again, **Whom seek ye?** And they said, Jesus of Nazareth, Jesus answered, **I have told you that I am he; If therefore ye seek me, let these go their way,** That the saying might be fulfilled, which he spake, **Of them which thou gavest me have I lost none, accept the one which betrayeth Me.**

Then came forth Judas, Simon's son, "That said and for a sign," the one who I shall kiss is he, hold him fast. And as soon as he was come, he goeth straightway to him, and saith, Master, master; and kiss him. Jesus said unto him, **Judas, betrayest thou the Son of man with a kiss?**

Then they laid their hands on him, to take him: But Simon Peter having a sword drew it, and smote the high priest's servant, cutting off his right ear, the servants name was Malchus. Then said Jesus unto Peter, **Put up thy sword into the sheath: all who take up the sword shall perish with the sword, for the cup which my Father, hath given me, shall I not drink of it? Know thou not that I can pray unto my Father, and he shall presciently give me more than twelve legions** of angels; **But how then shall the scriptures be fulfilled, that thus it must be?** And he touched his ear, and healed him. Jesus answered them, **I spake openly to the world; I ever taught in the synagogues and the temple, and in secret have I said nothing. But ye come out against me as a thief, with swords and staves? When I was daily with you in the temple. Ye stretched forth no hands against me: But this is your hour, and the power of darkness, is at hand.**

And they all forsook him, and fled. And there followed him a certain young man, having a linen cloth cast about his body, and the young men laid hold upon him; and he left the linen cloth, and fled, from them naked.

Peter's First Denial

And Simon Peter followed Jesus, and the disciple that was known unto the high priest, and so did another disciple: went in with Jesus into the palace of the high priest. But Peter stood at the door without. Then went out that other disciple, and spake unto her that kept the door, and brought in Peter. Then she said unto him, art not thou also one of this man's disciples? He saith, I am not. And the servants and officers that were there, made a fire of coals; for it was cold: and they warmed themselves: and Peter stood with them, warming himself also.

Annas Questions Jesus

Then the band and the captain and officers of the Jews took Jesus, and bound him, and led him away first to Annas; for he was father in law to Caiaphas, which was the high priest that same year. Now Caiaphas was he, which gave counsel to the Jews, that it was expedient that one man should die for the people.

The high priest then asked Jesus of his disciples, and of his doctrine. Jesus answered him, **I spake openly to the world; I ever taught in the synagogue, and in the temple, whither the Jews always resort; and in secret have I said nothing. Why askest thou me? ask them which heard me, what I have said unto them: behold, they know what I said.** And when he had thus spoken, one of the officers which stood by struck Jesus with the palm of his hand, saying, Answerest thou the high priest so? Jesus answered him, **If I have spoken evil, bear witness of the evil: but if well, why smitest thou me?** Then Annas had sent him bound unto Caiaphas the high priest.

CAIAPHAS QUESTIONS JESUS

And they laid hold on Jesus led him away to Caiaphas palace, the high priest, where the scribes, elders and chief priests were assembled. And Peter followed him afar off, even unto the palace of the high priest: and he sat with the servants, and warmed himself at the fire, to see the end.

And the chief priests, and elders, and all the council, sought for witness against Jesus to put him to death; But found none: yea, though many false witnesses came, yet found they none. At the last came two false witnesses, and bare witness against him, saying, we heard him say, I will destroy this temple that is made with human hands, and within three days I will build another made without hands. But neither so did their witness agree together.

And the high priest arose, up in the midst, and said unto him, Answerest thou nothing? What is it which these witness against thee? But he held his peace. Then high priest asked him, Art thou the Christ? **If I tell you, ye will not believe: And if I also ask you, ye will not answer me, nor let me go.**

Then he again, said unto him, I adjure thee by the living God, that thou tell us whether thou be the Christ, the Son of the God, Blessed? And Jesus said, **(I Am:) nevertheless I say unto you, Hereafter shall ye see the Son of man sitting on the right hand of power, and coming in the clouds of heaven.** Then the high priest rent his clothes, and saith, what need we any further witnesses? Behold, now ye have heard his blasphemy. What think ye? They answered and said,

He is guilty of death. And some began to spit on him, and to cover his face, and to buffet him, striking him with the palms of their hands and to say unto him, Prophesy: unto us thou Christ, who is he that smote thee?

Peter's Denial

And as Peter was beneath in the palace, where they had kindled a fire in the midst of the hall, for the night was cold, and they were all sat down together, Peter also sat down among them. There cometh one of the maids of the high priest: and saw Peter sitting warming himself, she looked earnestly, upon him, and said, Thou also was with Jesus of Nazareth. But he denied, saying, Woman I know him not, neither understand what thou sayest: But she said again, this fellow was with Jesus, for he also is a Galilean, for thou speech bewrayeth ye: But again he denied with an oath, I do not know the man, and the cock crewed. And after about the space of one hour, another came, that stood by, one of the servants of the high priest, being his kinsman of whose ear Peter had cut off, saith, Of a truth this fellow also was one of them, did not I see thee in the garden with him? Then Peter began to curse, and swear, Man I know not the man, of whom ye speakth. And while he yet spake, the cock crewed again, Jesus turned, and looked upon him. And Peter remembered the word of the Lord, which said unto him, **Before the cock crows, twice thou shalt deny me thrice.**

Peter went out, and wept bitterly.

Religious Leaders Send Jesus to Pilate

The Death of Judas

And as soon as it was morning, all the chief priests and elders of the people took counsel against Jesus to put him to death: Then when they had bound him, they led him away, and delivered him unto Pontius Pilate the governor.

Then Judas, his betrayer, seeing that Jesus had been condemned, was remorseful and brought back the thirty pieces of silver to the chief priests and elders, saying, "I have sinned by betraying innocent blood."

And they said, "What *is that* unto us? You see *to it!*"

Then he threw down the pieces of silver in the temple and departed, went out and hanged himself. But the chief priests took the silver pieces and saith, "It is not lawful to put them into the treasury, because they are the price of blood." And they consulted together and bought with them the potter's field, to bury strangers in. Therefore that field has been called the Field of Blood unto this day.

Then was fulfilled what was spoken by Jeremiah the prophet, saying, *"And they took the thirty pieces of silver, the value of Him who was betraide, whom they of the children of Israel priced, and gave them for the potter's field, as the Lord directed me."*

TRIAL FOR PILATE

Then Pilate entered into the judgment hall, being governor: And Jesus stood before him. And the chief priests accused him of many things: But he answerest nothing. Then they began saying, we found this fellow perverting the nation, and forbidding to give tribute unto Caesar, saying that he himself is Christ a King. And Pilate asked him saying, Answerest thou nothing? Behold how many things they witness against thee, But Jesus yet answered nothing; so that Pilate marvelled.

Then Pilate asked him, saying, Art thou the King of the Jews? Jesus answered him, **Sayest thou this thing of thy self, or did others tell it unto thee of me?** Pilate answered, Am I a Jew? thine own nation and the chief priests have delivered thee unto me: what hast thou done? Jesus answered, **My kingdom is not of this world: if my kingdom were of this world, then would my servants fight, that I should not be delivered unto the Jews: but now is my kingdom not from hence.** Pilate therefore said unto him, Then You are a king! Jesus answered, **"I AM" To this end was I born, and for this cause came I into the world, that I should bear witness unto the (truth). Every one that is of the truth hearth my voice,** Pilate said (what is truth).

Then when he had called together the chief priests and the rulers of the people, said he unto them, Ye have brought this man unto me, as one that perverteth the people: and, behold, I, having examined him before you, and have found no fault in this man, touching those things where of ye accuse him of before me. And I have found nothing worthy of death in him. I will therefore chastise him, and release him.

They answered and said unto him, if he were not a malefactor, we would not have delivered him up unto thee. Then Pilate said unto them, Take ye him, and judge him according unto or own your law. The Jews therefore said unto him, It is not lawful for us to put any man to death: That the saying of Jesus might be fulfilled, which he spake, signifying what death he should die. And they were the more fierce, saying, He stirreth up the people, teaching throughout all Jewry, beginning from Galilee to this place. Pilate again said I find no fault in this man; Take ye him, and crucify him:

Jesus before Herod

When Pilate heard Jesus was from Galilee, he asked whether the man were a Galilaean. And as soon as it was made know unto him, that he belonged unto Herod's jurisdiction, he sent him unto Herod, who himself also was at Jerusalem at that time. And when Herod saw Jesus, he was exceeding glad: for he was desirous to see him of a long season, because he had heard many things of him; and he hoped to have seen some miracle done by him.

Then he questioned with him in many words; but Jesus answered him nothing. And the chief priests and scribes stood and vehemently accused him. And Herod with his men of war set him at nought, and mocked him, and arrayed him in a gorgeous robe, and sent him again to Pilate. And that same day Pilate and Herod were made friends together: for before they were at enmity between themselves.

And then Pilate, when he had called together the chief priests and the rulers and the people, said unto them, Ye have brought this man unto me, as one that perverteth the people: and, behold, I, having examined him before you, and have found no fault in this man touching those things whereof ye accuse him: No, nor yet Herod: for I sent you to him; and, lo, nothing worthy of death has been by done by him. I will therefore chastise him, and release him.

The Sentence of Death

He went out again unto the Jews that were gathered together, and said unto them, I find in him no fault at all. And when, he was set down upon the judgment seat, His wife sent unto him, saying, Have thou nothing to do with that just man: for I have suffered many things this day in a dream because of him. Then Pilate said, Take ye him, and crucify him: for I find no fault in him. Then the Jews answered him, We have a law, and by our law he ought to die, because he made himself the Son of God. When Pilate therefore heard that saying, he was the more afraid;

Again Pilate went to Jesus, and saith unto Him. Who art thou? But Jesus gave him no answer. Then saith Pilate unto him, Speakest thou not unto me? Knowest thou not that I have power to crucify thee, and have power to release thee? Jesus answered, **Thou couldest have no power at all against me, except it were given thee from above: therefore he that delivered me unto thee hath the greater sin.** And from thenceforth Pilate sought to release him: but the Jews cried out, saying, If thou let this man go, thou art not Caesars friend: whosoever maketh himself a king speaketh against Caesar.

Pilate thus said unto them. For I know that ye have a custom, that I should release unto you one at the Passover. Barnabas, which lay bound with them that had made insurrection with him, who had committed murder.

Or Jesus which is called the Christ the King of the Jews, for he knew that for envy they had delivered him. But the chief priests and elders persuaded the multitude that they should ask for Barnabas and have Jesus put to death.

When Pilate therefore heard that saying, he brought Jesus forth, and sat down again in the judgment seat in a place that is called the Pavement, but in Hebrew, Gabbatha. And it was the preparation of the passover, and about sixth hour: and he saith unto the Jews, Behold your King! But they cried out, Away with him, away with Him, crucify him. Pilate saith the third time, Why what evil hath he done? Shall I crucify your king? The chief priests answered, We have no king but Caesar. And the voices of them and of the chief priests prevailed.

When Pilate saw that it was hopeless, but that rather a tumult was made, he took water, and washed his hands before the multitude, saying, I am innocent of the blood of this just person: see ye to it. And gave sentence that it should be as they required. Then answered the people, and said, May His blood be upon us, and on our children. So he released Barnabas unto them: and when he had scourged Jesus, he delivered him to be crucified.

MOCKING BY SOLDIERS

And the soldiers of the governor lead him into the common hall, called Praetorium; and there gathered unto him the whole band of soldiers. Then they stripped him, and put on him a scarlet robe. And when they had fashioned a crown of thorns, they put it upon his head: and bowed the knee before him, saying, Hail King of the Jews! Then they spit upon him, and took the reed, and smote him on the head. And after that they had mocked him, they took the robe off from him, and put his own raiment on him, and led him away to crucify him.

The Road to Golgotha; The Crucifixion

And as they came out they laid hold upon one Simon, of Cyrenian, who was coming out of the country, the father of Alexander and Rufus, and compelled him to bear the cross. For Jesus being to weaken to bear the cross. And he bearing his cross went forth into a place called the skull, which is called in Hebrew Golgotha: And there followed him a great company of people, and of women, which also bewailed and lamented him.

But Jesus turning unto them said, **Daughters of Jerusalem, weep not for me, but weep for yourselves, and for your children. For, behold the days are coming, in the which they shall say, Blessed are the barren, and the wombs that never bare, and the paps which never gave suck. Then shall they begin to say unto the mountains, Fall upon us; and the hills, Cover us. For if they do these things then the tree is green, what shall be done in the dry?** And there were also two malefactors, lead away with him to be put to death. As the scripture was fulfilled, which saith**, *And he was numbered with the transgressors.***

When they were come unto the place, they gave him vinegar to drink mingled with gall: and when he had tasted thereof he would not drink of it.

At Calvary, There they crucified him, and the malefactors, one on the right hand, the other on the left. It was the ninth hour:

And Pilate wrote on a title, and put it on the cross. And the writing was,(***Jesus of Nazareth the King of the Jews***).

This then was read by many of the Jews: for the place where Jesus was crucified was nigh unto the city: and it was written in Hebrew, and Greek, and Latin. Then saith the chief priests of the Jews to Pilate, Write not, the King of the Jews; but that he said, I am King of the Jews. Pilate answered, What I have written I have written.

Then the soldiers, when they had crucified Jesus, took his garments, and make four parts, to every soldier a part; and also took his coat: now the coat was without seam, woven from the top throughout by his mother. They saith therefore among themselves, Let us not rend it, but cast lots for it, to see whose it shall be: that the scripture might be fulfilled, which sayth, *They parted my raiment among them, and for my vesture they did cast lots.* These things therefore the soldiers did.

And they that passed by reviled him, wagging their heads, and saying, Thou that destroyest the temple, and buildest it in three days, save thyself. If thou be the Son of God, come down from the cross. He saved others; himself he cannot save, If he be the King of Israel, let him now come down from the cross, and we will believe him.

He trusted in God; let him deliver him now, if he will have him; for he said," I am the son of God". Likewise also the chief priests, mocking said among themselves with the scribes, the same things.

And one of the malefactors which were hanged railed on him, saying, If thou be Christ, save thyself and us. But the other answering rebuked him, saying, Dost not thou fear God, seeing thou art in the same condemnation? We indeed are justly; receiving the due reward of our deeds: but this man hath done nothing amiss. And he said unto *Jesus, Lord,* remember me when thou comest into thy kingdom. And Jesus said unto him, **Verily I say unto thee, Today shalt thou be with me in paradise.**

The Death on the Cross; The Burial of Jesus

And it was about the sixth hour, and there was a darkness over all the earth until the ninth hour. Jesus cried with a loud voice, saying, ***Eloi, Eloi, Lama Sabachthani?*** Which is, being interpreted, **My God, my God, why hast thou forsaken me?** And some of them that stood by, heard it, and said, Behold, he calleth Elias.

Now there stood by the cross of Jesus his mother, and his mother's sister, Mary the wife of Cleophas, and Mary Magdalene. When Jesus therefore saw his mother, and the disciple, John, standing by, whom he loved, he saith unto his mother, **Woman, beholdth thy son!** Then saith he unto the disciple, **Behold thy mother!** And from that hour that disciple took her unto his own home.

Jesus then said: **Father forgiveth them for they no not what they do.** After this, Jesus knowing all things were now accomplished, that the scripture might be fulfilled, saith, **I thirst.** Now there was set a vessel full of vinegar; and straightway one of them ran, and took a sponge, filled it with vinegar, and put it on a reed, lifting it to his mouth and gave him to drink. The rest said, Leave him alone, let us see whether Elias will come to saveth him.

When Jesus therefore had received the vinegar, he said, ***It is Finished"*** **"Father into thy hands I commend my spirit: and he cried out, bowed his head, and gave up His Ghost.**

And all the people that came together to that sight, beholding the things which were done, smote their breasts, and returned home. And, behold, the veil of the temple was rent in twain from the top to the bottom; and the earth did quake, and the rocks rent; and the graves were opened; and many bodies of the saints which slept arose, and came out of the graves after his resurrection, and went into the holy city, and appeared unto many.

Now when the centurion, and they that were with him, watching Jesus, saw the earthquake, and those things that were done, feared greatly, glorifying God, saying, ***"Truly this was a righteous man, the Son of God:***

Know therefore the Jews said, because it was the preparation day, that the bodies should not remain upon the cross on the sabbath day, (for the sabbath was an high day.)

Then the religious leaders besought Pilate that their legs might be broken, and that they might be taken away. Then came the soldiers, and broke the legs of the first, and of the other which was crucified with him. But when they came to Jesus, they saw he was already dead, but one of the soldiers with a spear in hand came forth pierced his side, and forthwith came there out blood and water.

And he that saw it, bare record, that the record is true: that ye might believe. For these things were done, that the scripture should be fulfilled, *A bone of him shall not be broken.* And again another scripture saith, *They shall look on him whom they pierced.*

And many women were their beholding afar off, which followed Jesus from Galilee, came ministering unto him: Among which was Mary Magdalene, and Mary the mother of James and Joses, and the mother of Zebedees children and Salome;

JESUS IS LAID IN THE TOMB

When the even was come, there came a rich man of Arimathaea, named Joseph, an honorable counselor, and a disciple of Jesus, which also waited for the kingdom of God, came, and went in boldly unto Pilate, and begged the body of Jesus. And Pilate marveled if he were already dead: and calling unto him the centurion, he asked him whether he was already dead or not? And when he knew of it, he gave the centurion orders that the boby of Jesus should be taken down and given to Joseph. And he bought fine linen, and took him and wrapped him in the linen, and laid him in His own sepulcher which was hewn out of a rock. And rolled a stone unto the door of the sepulcher. And Mary Magdalene and Mary the mother of Joses beheld where he was laid. And they returned, and prepared spices and ointments; and rested on the Sabbath day according to the commandment. Now there came also Nicodemus, which at the first came to Jesus by night, and brought a mixture of myrrh and aloes, about a hundred pound weight.

Guards Are Posted At the Tomb

On the next day, which followed the day of preparation, the chief priests and Pharisees gathered together unto Pilate, saying, "Sir, we remember, while He was still alive, how that deceiver said, 'After three days I will rise.' Therefore command that the tomb be made secure until the third day, lest His disciples come by night and steal Him away, and say unto the people, 'He has risen from the dead.' So the last deception will be worse than the first." Pilate said unto them, "You have a guard; go your way, make *it* as secure as ye know how." So they went and made the tomb secure, sealing the stone and setting the guard.

The Empty Tomb

And when the Sabbath was past, on the first day of the week, very early in the morning, while it was still dark. Mary Magdalene, and Mary the mother of James, and Salome, were bringing the spices which they had prepared, and certain others with them. And they said among themselves, Who shall roll away for us the stone from the door of the sepulcher? Just then there was a great earthquake: for the angel of the Lord descended from heaven, and came and rolled back the stone from the door, and sat upon it. His countenance was liken as unto lightning, and his raiment white as snow: And for fear of him the keepers did shake, and became as dead men. And as the women neared the tomb they looked and they saw that the stone was rolled away, And then as they enter into the sepulcher, they saw two young men standing one at the head were they laid Jesus and other at the foot clothed in long white robes and they were afraid, and bowed down their faces to the earth.

But Mary stood without at the sepulcher weeping: and as she wept, she stooped down, and looked into the sepulcher and seeth the two angels in white, and where the body of Jesus had lain, The angels said unto them, *why seek ye the living among the dead. He is not here, but is risen: remember how he spake unto you when he was in Galilee, saying, The Son of man must be delivered into the hands of sinful men, and be crucified, and the third day rise again,* and they remembered his word.

Then the Angel saith unto them, *Go your way, tell his disciple what you have seen and heard, he is risen from the dead; For behold he goeth before you into Galilee; there shall ye see him: lo, I have told you.*

Jesus Appears to Mary Magdalene

Quickly, they fled from the sepulcher; for they trembled and were amazed: Neither said they to any man. And as they were on their way Jesus met Mary Magdalene, out of whom he had cast the seven devils, saying, All hail, she turned about and saw him, who said unto her, **Woman, why weepiest thou?** She, supposing him to be the gardener, said unto him, Sir, if thou have borne him hence, tell me where thou hast laid him, and I will take him away. Jesus saith unto her, **Mary,** and she said unto him, Rabboni; which is to say, Master. Jesus saith unto her, **Touch me not; for I am not yet ascended unto my Father: but go to my brethren, and say to them, I ascend unto my Father, and your Father; and to my God, and your God.** She fell down and worshipped him by his feet.

So she went forth and joined the others, going their way and came unto the disciples telling them what they had seen and heard from the Lord, and that he had spoken these things unto them. That He is risen: and to tell my brethren that they should go into Galilee. And there shall they see me.

And the apostles believed them not, their words; seemed to them as idle tales. Then arose Peter, went forth, and one of the other disciples, so they ran both together: and the other disciple did outrun Peter, and came first to the sepulchre. And he stooping down, looked in, and saw the linen clothes lying; but went he not in. Then cometh Simon Peter following him. And went into the sepulchre, and seeth the linen clothes lie, and the napkin, that was about his head, not lying with the linen clothes, but wrapped together in a place by itself. Then went in also that other disciple, which came first to the sepulchre, and he saw, and believed. And they departed, wondering in themselves at that which was come to pass. And went their way unto Galilee.

The Bribing Of the Roman Soldiers

Now when they were going, behold, some of the watch came into the city, and showed unto the chief priests all the things that were done. And when they were assembled with the elders, and had taken counsel, they gave a large amount of money unto the soldiers, saying, Say ye, His disciples came by night, and stole him away while we slept. And if this come to the governor's ears, we will persuade him, and secure you. So they took the money, and did as they were taught: and this saying is commonly reported among the Jews until this day.

JESUS APPEARS TO THE TWO MEN ON THE ROAD

And, behold, Jesus appeared in another form unto two of them who went that same day unto a village called Emmaus, which was from Jerusalem about threescore furlongs. And they talked together of all these things which had happened. And it came to pass, that, while they communed together and reasoned, Jesus himself droth near, and walk with them. But their eyes were holden that they should not know him. And he said unto them, **What manner of communications are these that ye have one to another, as ye walk, and are sadden?** And the one of them, whose name was Cleopas, answering said unto him, Art thou only a stranger in Jerusalem, and hast not known the things which are come to pass there in these days? And he said unto them, **What things?** And they said unto him, Concerning Jesus of Nazareth, which was a prophet mighty in deed and word before God and all the people: And how the chief priests and our rulers delivered him to be condemned to death, and have crucified him.

But we trusted that it had been he which should have redeemed Israel: and beside all this, today is the third day since these things were done. Yea, and certain women also of our company made us astonished, which were early at the sepulchre; And when they found not his body, they came, saying, that they had also seen a vision of angels, which said that he was alive.

And two of his disciples which were with us went to the sepulchre, and found *it* even so as the women had said: but him they saw not. Then he said unto them, **O fools, and slow of heart to believe all that**

the prophets have spoken: Ought not Christ to have suffered these things, and to enter into his glory? And beginning at Moses and all the prophets, he expounded unto them in all the scriptures the things concerning himself. And they drew nigh unto the village, whither they went: and he made as though he would have gone further. But they constrained him, saying, Abide with us: for it is toward evening, and the day is far spent. He went in to tarry with them. And it came to pass, as he sat at meat with them, he took bread, and blessed *it*, and

broke it, and gave unto them. And their eyes were opened, and they knew him; and he vanished out of their sight. And they said one to another, Did not our heart burn within us, while he talked with us by the way, and while he opened unto us the scriptures? And they rose up the same hour, and returned to Jerusalem, and found the eleven gathered together, and they that were with them, saying, The Lord is risen indeed, and hath appeared unto us.

Jesus Appears to His Disciples Behind Locked Doors

After, the two men came and told what things were done in the way, and how he was made known unto them in the breaking of bread. That the same day at evening, being the first day of the week, when the doors were shut, where the disciples were assembled for fear of the Jews, came Jesus himself and stood in their midst, and saith unto them, saying, **Peace be unto you**. But they were terrified and affrighted, and supposed that they had seen a spirit. And he said unto them, **Why are ye troubled? And why do those thoughts arise with in your hearts? Behold my hands and my feet, that it is I myself: handle me, and see; for a spirit hath not flesh nor bones, as ye see me have.** And when he had thus spoken, he showed them his side, and his hands and feet. And while they yet believed not for joy, and wondered, He saith unto them, **Have ye here any meat?** And they gave him a peace of a broiled fish, and of an honeycomb. And he took it, and did eat before them. Then Jesus said to them again, **Peace be unto you: as my Father hath sent me, even so send I you.** And when he had thus said this, He said unto them, **Whose soever sins ye remit, they are remitted unto them; and whose soever sins ye retain, they are retained.**

Jesus Appeared to Thomas

But Thomas, one of the twelve, called Didymus, was not with them when Jesus came. The other disciples therefore said unto him, we have seen the Lord. But he said unto them, Except I shall see in his hands the print of the nails, and put my finger into them, and thrust my hand into his side, I will not believe.

And after eight days again his disciples were within, and Thomas was with them: then came Jesus, the doors being shut, and stood in their midst, and said, **Peace be unto you. Then saith he to Thomas, Reach hither thy finger, and behold my hands; and reach hither thy hand, and thrust it into my side: and be not faithless, but believing.** And Thomas answered and said unto him, *My Lord and my God.* Jesus saith unto him, **Thomas, because thou hast seen me, thou hast believed: blessed are they that have not seen, and yet have believed.** And many other signs truly did Jesus in the presence of his disciples.

JESUS APPEARS TO THE DISCIPLES WHILE THEY FISHED

After these things Jesus showed himself again to the disciples at the sea of Tiberias; and on this wise showed he himself. There were together *Simon Peter*, and *Thomas* called Didymus, and *Nathanael* of Cana in Galilee, and the sons of Zebedee, and two other of his disciples. Simon Peter saith unto them, I go a fishing. They said unto him, we also go with thee. They went forth, and entered into a ship immediately; and that night they caught nothing. But when the morning was now come, Jesus stood on the shore: but the disciples knew not that it was Jesus. Then Jesus saith unto them, **Children, have ye any meat?** They answered him, no. And he said unto them, **Cast the net on the right side of the ship, and ye shall find**. They cast therefore, and now they were not able to draw it for the multitude of fishes.

Therefore that disciple whom Jesus loved saith unto Peter, It is the Lord. Now when Simon Peter heard that it was the Lord, he girt his fisher's coat unto him, (for he was naked,) and did cast himself into the sea. And the other disciples came in on the little ship; (for they were not far from land, but as it were two hundred cubits,) dragging the net with the fishes. As soon then as they were come to land, they saw a fire of coals there, and fish laid thereon, and bread.

Jesus saith unto them, **Bring of the fish which ye have now caught.** Simon Peter went up, and drew the net to land full of great fishes, an hundred and fifty and three: and for all there were so many, yet was not the net broken. Jesus saith unto them, **Come and dine.** And none of the disciples durst ask him, Who art thou? knowing that it was the Lord. Jesus then cometh, and taketh bread, and giveth unto them, and the fish likewise. This is now the third time that Jesus showed himself to his disciples, after that he was risen from the dead.

Jesus Talks with Peter

So when they had dined, Jesus saith unto Simon Peter, **Simon, son of Jonas, lovest thou me more than these?** He said unto him, Yea, Lord; thou knowest that I love thee. He saith unto him, **Feed my lambs.** He saith to him again the second time, **Simon, son of Jonas, lovest thou me?** He said unto him, Yea, Lord; thou knowest that I love thee. He saith unto him, **Feed my sheep.** Again saith unto him the third time, **Simon, son of Jonas, lovest thou me?** Peter was grieved because he said unto him the third time, Lovest thou me? And he said unto him, Lord, thou knowest all things; and knowest that I love thee. Jesus saith unto him, **Feed my sheep. Verily, verily, I say unto thee, When thou wast young, thou girdest thyself, and walkedst whither thou wouldest: but when thou shalt be old, thou shalt stretch forth thy hands, and another shall gird thee, and carry thee whither thou wouldest not.** This spake he, signifying by what death he should glorify God. And when he had spoken this, he saith unto him, **Follow me.**

Then Peter, turning about, seeth the disciple whom Jesus loved following; which also leaned on his breast at the last supper, and said, Lord, which is he that betrayeth thee? Peter seeing him said to Jesus, Lord, and what shall this man do? Jesus saith unto him, **If I will that he tarry till I come, what is that to thee? follow thou me.** Then went this saying abroad among the brethren, that that disciple should not die: yet Jesus said not unto him, He shall not die; but, if I will that he tarry till I come, what is that to thee? This is the disciple which testifieth of these things, and wrote these things: and we know that his testimony is true. And there are also many other things which Jesus did, the which, if they should be written every one, I suppose that even the world itself could not contain the books that should be written. Amen.

Jesus Gives The Great Commission

Then the eleven disciples went away into Galilee, unto a mountain where Jesus had appointed them. And when they saw him, they worshipped him: but some doubted. And Jesus came and spake unto them, saying,

All Power is given unto me in heaven and in earth. Go ye into the all the world, and preach the gospel to every creature, and to all nations, baptizing them in the name of the Father, and the Son, and of the Holy Ghost: He that believeth and is baptized shall be saved; but he that believeth not shall be condemned. Teaching them to observe all things whatsoever I have commanded you: And these signs shall follow them that believe; In my name shall they cast out devils; they shall speak with new tongues; They shall take up serpents; and if they drink any deadly thing, it shall not hurt them; they shall lay hands on the sick, and they shall recover.

Jesus Appears To the Disciples in Jerusalem

These are the words which I spoken unto you, while I was yet with you, that all things must be fulfilled, which were written in the law of Moses, and in the prophets, and in the psalms, concerning me. Then opened he their understanding, that they might understand the scriptures, and said unto them,

Thus it is written, and thus it behooved Christ to suffer, and to rise from the dead the third day: And that repentance and remission of sins should be preached in his name among all nations, beginning at Jerusalem. And ye are witnesses of all these things. And, behold, I send the promise of my Father upon you: but tarry ye in the city of Jerusalem, until ye be endued with power from on high.

JESUS ASCENDS INTO HEAVEN

And being assembled together with them, He commanded them not to depart from Jerusalem, but to wait for the Promise of the Father, "which," *He said.*

What you have heard from Me; for John truly baptized with water, but you shall be baptized with the Holy Spirit, not many days from now." Therefore, when they had come together, they asked Him, saying, "Lord, will You at this time restore the kingdom to Israel?" And He said unto them, **"It is not for you to know times or seasons which the Father has put in His own authority. But ye shall receive power when the Holy Spirit has comth upon you; and ye shall be witnesses unto Me in Jerusalem, and in all Judea and Samaria, and to the end's of the earth." Lo, I am with you always, even unto the end of the world.**

So then after the Lord had spoken these things, unto them, he led them out as far as to Bethany, and he lifted up his hands, and blessed them. And while they looked steadfastly toward heaven, he was parted from them, and was carried up into heaven and a cloud received, Him out of their sight. To be seated at the right hand of God. And behold, two men stood by them in white apparel, saying *"Men of Galilee, why do you stand gazing up into heaven? This same Jesus, who was taken up from you into heaven, will so come in like manner as you saw Him go into heaven. "* Then they worshiped

Him, and went forth preaching all things the Lord said unto them.

Then they returned to Jerusalem from the mount called Olivet, which is near Jerusalem, a Sabbath day's journey. And when they had entered, they went up into the upper room where they were staying: ***Peter, James, John, and Andrew; Philip*** and ***Thomas; Bartholomew and Matthew; James*** *the son* of Alphaeus and ***Simon*** the Zealot; and ***Judas*** *the son* of James. These all continued with one accord in prayer and supplication, with great joy. And were continually in the temple, praising and blessing God. Waiting, for the Holy Spirit, with the women and Mary the mother of Jesus, and with His brothers.

INDEX

www.ingramcontent.com/pod-product-compliance
Lightning Source LLC
Chambersburg PA
CBHW030908120626
46554CB00001B/58